THE
IMPACT
TRIANGLE

Printed in the United States of America

First Printing, 2013

ISBN 978-0-9896846-0-6

Library of Congress Control Number: 2013914530

Published by
Hiapo Press
10250 Rancho Carmel Drive
San Diego , CA
858.618.4762

Copy edited by Lisa Wolff
Indexed by Ken Della Penta
Designed by Faceout Studio

THE
IMPACT
TRIANGLE

THE 3 ESSENTIALS TO ACCELERATE
YOUR NONPROFIT ENTERPRISE

— CINDI PHALLEN —

HIAPO
PRESS

This book is dedicated to Ikaika.

"I love you more than life itself."

ACKNOWLEDGMENTS

I WANT TO THANK MY wonderful friends around the country who have served as a second family, who have not just inspired me, but made me feel supported and capable during the past year. You know who you are…

And my family who cheered me on, even when I'm sure they thought I was nuts. Thanks, Steve, for all the IT assistance! Mom and Dad, for the safety net and for telling me I'm smart ☺. Pam, for embracing the idea even when I couldn't articulate it yet.

Corey, you are always at least part of the reason I do anything.

To Betsy, Claudia, Renee, and Lazon—the best friends from GNO, who have stood beside me for over a decade.

To the Rogers family, my West Coast family, who adopted me and little cp.

To Eryn, who changed my mindset permanently in ways hard to express. Thank you for the inspiration.

To these wonderful mentors:

Steve O'Kane, who was put in an impossible situation and never wavered.

Dick Chapel, whose patience and brilliance guided and taught me so much, and whose unconditional support is always felt.

Rich Collato, whose wisdom, advice, and confidence in me has launched me forward and changed me for the better.

To Team CP—Bill Davis, David Narevsky, David Robertson, Ray Schnorr, and Ursula Walsh—the advisors who watched me flounder, who never laughed at me, only with me; who encouraged, advised, scolded, and picked me up. Your willingness to push me through is beyond reasonable expectations.

To Mary Andrews and Marilyn King, my coaches and friends—I'm still trying to absorb the fact that I have two Olympians in my corner, after all these years! Much gratitude...

To Lenore Lowe, for encouraging me, challenging me, teaching me, and providing an occasional reality check.

A special shout out to Laurie McLoughlin, who seemed as excited about the creation of this book as I was! Thanks for all the lunch conversations and brainstorming.

To Alfredo....similar journeys....similar results....kindred spirits...I remain always grateful to you.

To Karla Olson—if it weren't for your genius and encouragement, this book would still be on my laptop!

The rest of you—thank you for being part of my village. We will march on together, laughing all the way!

TABLE OF CONTENTS

Part Four: Applying the Impact Triangle to Fund Development

Part Five: Applying the Impact Triangle to Building the Potential in Staff

Part Six: The Benefits of the Impact Triangle…and the Real Secret

PART ONE

THE IMPACT TRIANGLE

CHAPTER ONE

WHAT IS THE IMPACT TRIANGLE?

AS A NONPROFIT LEADER, there comes a moment in your life when you know you are in trouble.

Mine came about half an hour after the end of a terrific event where we were celebrating the ground-breaking of a new facility. The turnout was better than expected; my marketing plan had worked. The speakers had kept to the schedule; my detailed organization ran like clockwork. When the shovels hit the ground, there was tangible excitement about this new period of growth that would have remarkable impact on the community; it was just as I'd imagined. I had everything to be proud of and I was jubilant—until I realized that I was in trouble. As I dragged chairs to storage and wiped down the kitchen, my elation evaporated because I was alone. Where was my team? Why, on this all-important day of celebration, was there no one there with me? *Uh-oh.*

I finished closing up, and as I was walking up the street to my car, I admitted to myself that I had missed the boat somewhere. I acknowledged that if I took an honest look at how things had been going, I would have to admit that very few of the people who worked with me were engaged in the real work. While working so hard, putting in long hours, I thought that I had been applying best practices. I was so busy worrying about the details and the schedules that I didn't have time to work with the board, finish those training plans for staff, complete the annual fundraising plan, or even respond to the new police chief in town who had asked for a meeting. I was plugging away and missing the big picture.

I sat in my car for a minute and took a few deep breaths. I vowed that I would never find myself alone at the end of an event again. I decided that I would change my focus and find the solution, find the key, to running a sustainable, thriving organization that made deep community impact and was supported by many volunteers and staff. I wouldn't stop until I figured out how.

And I didn't.

In order to be strong organizations that are valued in the community, we need a different approach.

I suggest that you start by thinking of your nonprofit as a social enterprise. You are charged with ensuring there are resources to change the community, maybe even the world. You can't do that by having a scarcity mindset. By reading this book, you are taking an important step toward a deeper commitment to improving the work of your organization.

Those of us in the nonprofit world know what it's like to scramble for funding. We know how it feels to hold your breath to see who is going to step up and work alongside you. We may be ready to move the organization to the next level, but we aren't quite sure how to make it happen. We keep trying to get to that strategic plan, but with all the day-to-day details, there is never enough time.

On top of that, we've seen the confusion on board members' faces when they are unclear about their roles, and it feels like their efforts are wasted because the organization is stalled. We have been in that challenging transition period, when it is hard to focus on the most essential priorities. And we've witnessed staff settle into a lackadaisical mode, accepting mediocrity as the norm.

We've all seen it. The question is: how can we change it?

How is it possible to transform lives and have a positive impact on the community when you feel like everything around you is in a state of chaos? Yes, it can feel like an overwhelming struggle, but now I know it doesn't have to be.

After working in the nonprofit sector for many years, I'm here to help you. You have made the choice to work in an industry where you get to reap the rewards of your work by strengthening the community. It's such an important task, but so complicated. But I'm here to tell you that you can see your vision come alive without so much stress, or feeling like you're on that hamster wheel. In fact, you can do it with the joy, satisfaction, and fulfillment that is the reason you chose this profession. You can do it by shifting your focus from chaos and damage control to three essential things—The Impact Triangle.

After I vowed to find new answers as an executive director, I knew it was time to look at things differently if I really wanted to avoid feeling so stressed and alone in this work. I chose to be responsible for my future in the organization. I knew it might be challenging. But there is something special about taking risks and trying new things—it can be invigorating. Do things differently than they have been done in the past, and then you can expect different results.

Wouldn't it be nice to have a strong team of engaged volunteers and staff who are happy to support the organization? Wouldn't it be great to have a robust strategy for funding the organization, with diverse revenue streams that negate the worry of balancing the budget every year? And wouldn't it be rewarding to see the mission come alive every day?

By being bold enough to stop the cycle of chaos and stress, we can achieve extraordinary results. And extraordinary results will set you apart. So we must look at things differently now. No more talk about how hard it's been since the recession, about how there aren't enough resources, about how we can't find donors, about how there isn't time to strategize or plan, and so on.

I have discovered three things that are required to achieve amazing results, and they are the three components of the Impact Triangle:

1. Choosing the right mindset
2. Focusing on strategic relationships
3. Utilizing winning practices and tools

Mindset separates the champions from the others. Once you approach situations with a renewed outlook, you can focus on the relationships you have with the people who are best suited to work alongside you. To round out the Impact Triangle, the tools and winning practices will ground you in the foundational basics for success.

I have seen this ring true when observing extraordinary leaders. They have used the lessons from the recession to be innovative and stay ahead of the curve. They do not have a limiting mindset, nor do they ignore the power of relationships, nor are they sloppy with systems and resources. Their organizations are well run and are relevant. They have moved the plan from the shelf into real-world action and obtained strong results. Each person in the organization—employees and volunteers alike—strives to be successful in reaching goals, making a positive difference, and perhaps influencing change on a broad scale. Very rarely does this happen by accident.

When I started applying the Impact Triangle to the work I was doing, I received awards for outstanding program quality; I raised more money year over year, including during the recession; I became the "go-to" expert for developing strong boards; and board members and staff knew exactly what the vision and the annual goals were for the organization. And just as important, I was having a good time!

In this book I will outline why mindset, relationships, and using the best tools are critical, and then I will teach you how to apply them to the four areas that businesses with a social mission find most challenging:

- ▶ Planning
- ▶ Building strong boards
- ▶ Fundraising
- ▶ Staff management

Every nonprofit organization is different, and there is certainly more than one way to get the same result. So be bold enough to be original when applying the Impact Triangle. You may feel vulnerable or uncertain, and that's good, because moving outside your comfort zone is required to learn and grow. You can take some risks, and try new and challenging things, and still stay on the course for success.

If you are not feeling energized and truly happy about where your organization is now, you must act. And I will guide you, because mediocrity, and being typical, isn't good enough when the world is counting on you to deliver on multiple bottom lines. The Impact Triangle will show you how to lay a strong foundation that will transform your organization. It's not a dramatic change, but it's enough to make big impact.

I worked very hard, and made plenty of mistakes, until I figured out how to grow the organization and increase impact. Give yourself permission to look at things differently, and try new things. You can make subtle changes in your approach that will reap dramatic positive results. No more scrambling for funding or confused board members; no more ambivalent staff or irrelevant plans.

It's time to get excited about the possibilities again, transform your organization, and go make a difference. Leading an organization with a social mission is a challenge. Whether you are a board member or on the staff leadership team, it can feel overwhelming to work in such a noble field. Embrace the Impact Triangle, get clear about priorities, and start enjoying your work again.

CHAPTER TWO

WHAT NONPROFITS ARE NOT

WHEN I REFER TO NONPROFITS in this book, I am referring mostly to 501(c)(3) public benefit, charitable organizations. This includes human service organizations, hospitals and universities, and organizations for the arts the environment, etc. Donations to these organizations are tax deductible within allowable limits. There are other nonprofit organizations such as trade, associations, membership, and political organizations, etc. To qualify, they must provide a benefit to their members instead of the public. Nonprofits, in compliance with IRS rules, generally do not pay tax on income. (Be sure to read up on your state laws regarding sales tax, unrelated business income, etc.)

I have a confession: I can't stand the word *nonprofit* because of what it implies. My goal in life is to hear everyone start calling nonprofits social businesses or enterprises.

Nonprofits are not poor agencies with few resources. But why is that the first thing many people think? I recently gave a speech entitled "The Landscape of Nonprofits." I asked the crowd what they thought of when they heard the word *nonprofit*. Responses included (and I'm quoting, because I wrote them down) "poorly managed"; "raising money"; "always behind the curve"; "good work; poorly funded"; "there's too many of them"; "under-funded"; "grants"; "boards without a purpose," and other descriptions along the same lines.

I don't think I'll ever ask that question again—the responses were a little depressing. (At least someone said "good work"!) Is this how we want the social sector to be perceived? I hope not. By the time I was finished with the speech, I asked the audience if they were feeling any differently about nonprofits. There was a positive response, but it really got me thinking, and I realized the perception is brought about at least in part by nonprofit leaders themselves. Sometimes you can be your own worst enemy. It's time to get out of your way.

Nonprofits are social enterprises. They conduct business a little differently, and the business model is usually different from that of for-profit entities. But nonprofits are not poorly resourced organizations run by too few staff, or by untrained leaders. Nonprofits are exactly what you make them. If you are in the community begging for money, or indicating your business is anything but thriving, you are creating a negative impression. You probably don't intend to, but what would happen if you asked the same questions I did? I wonder if the responses would vary much.

Stop thinking in terms of scarcity and create abundance. If you feel your organization is falling behind, then focus on addressing those concerns, and ask for help from others if you aren't sure how to fix the problem. Your work is too important to not go all in toward extraordinary results. The Impact Triangle can be the change-maker.

Nonprofits are not businesses that are trying to break even, or trying to just not lose too much money. Nonprofit does NOT mean no profit at the end of the fiscal year. It is okay, and encouraged, to have a surplus, positive variance, profit—whatever you wish to call it. Then you can fund reserves, or buy that equipment you have been putting off, or invest in staff development, or meet other organizational needs. How can you create life-changing impact if you are committed to saving every dime so you don't make any money?

Think like an investor. I understand responsible spending, and I want you to understand that focusing on growth can reap much bigger rewards. (See chapter 19 on earned revenue.) Imagine what is possible if you change your mindset.

Nonprofits are not lacking direction, with clueless board members. You have worked hard to recruit the right leaders from the community who are committed to your goals. They are investing their talent and resources, and inviting their network to invest also. They lay out strategy and policy, and they sacrifice family time. Let's honor their commitment and leverage that good work. Sometimes you may get it wrong and have a person on the team who really isn't well suited for the work. This is a business—so manage your people as you would in a for-profit company. Find a role for which they are better suited, or thank them for their service at the end of the year, and you can both move on.

Nonprofit organizations' top priority is not fundraising. Raising funds may be an important part of the plan, but it's not the only thing nonprofits do. Remember—it's not about the organization; it's about the community. The top priority is developing a sustainable strategy to deliver the mission. So working to create smart partnerships, developing strong programs and services, creating a top-notch staff team, building strong boards, intentionally executing a strategic plan, committing resources for the work, and investing in infrastructure to ensure success—these are all components of a strong nonprofit. What if, instead of trying to sell yourself as a pitiful nonprofit in need of help, you sold yourself as a *social impact enterprise, looking for partners to join a winning team*? Which do you think would appeal more? Try saying out loud to yourself, "I am a leader in a thriving social impact enterprise—who wants to join this winning team?"

Nonprofits pump billions of dollars into the economy. They employ millions of people. They meet needs that no other company or government can or will meet. Over 25 percent of adults volunteer with nonprofits. There is an increasing need for them, so let's look carefully at how we perceive nonprofits and how you talk about the sector. If there were no nonprofit businesses, who would feed the hungry, educate our kids, or care for the sick? Each one of us is touched by a nonprofit organization, probably every day.

It is time to focus on the vision and articulate your message by telling a different story. I am providing you with the tools to do so. But shifting your mindset starts with you. You can do this—be proud!

CHAPTER THREE

MINDSET MATTERS

Have you ever thought:

If I only had more time, I could develop some great strategies.

When you could have thought:

I'm going to carve out a little time each week to identify priorities and lay out some action steps.

Have you ever thought:

When are people going to stop bringing all their problems to me?

When you could have thought:

It's worth my time to be sure I've provided others with the resources to support our goals.

Have you ever thought:

There is just not enough money for that this month.

When you could have thought:

Let's look at alternatives that will still move us forward.

As these examples show, successful nonprofit leaders approach their work differently than those who consistently struggle. They have a different mindset; they think differently. *They do not form limiting beliefs before they experience the work.*

One component of a healthy perspective is setting a goal that has energy for you and believing it is possible to achieve. Success starts here. You may not be sure how it will come to fruition, or what the strategy is at the beginning, but you know it is worth pursuing.

Well, here's the good news: by continuing to envision the goal while being fully aware of your current state, your brain goes to work to identify key elements of a strategy, the steps that would have to occur in order to achieve that goal. The creative part of the brain is engaged. And here is what's interesting: even if you don't know how it will work, it doesn't matter. You will figure out that part. You must start by believing in your goal enough to persevere. You must know that you can make it happen.

A great example of this is two-time Olympian Marilyn King. While training for her third Olympic team in track and field, Marilyn's car was hit by a truck. She suffered a back injury that made it impossible for her to train physically for seven months. Using only mental training, such as visualization and goal-setting, she placed second at the Olympic Trials for the 1980 Moscow Games.

Clearly something amazing had occurred that prompted Marilyn's research and a thirty-year career in the field of exceptional human performance. One of the things she learned was the impact of what and how we think about our health, our performance, and our future. She went on to create Olympian Thinking™ with corporate leadership teams, youth educators, and thought leaders in the evolution of peace. To learn more about Marilyn's work and secrets of high performance, visit www.waybeyondsports.com.

When you start thinking about how you are thinking, that is the first step toward success. Your approach sets the tone.

Anything Is Possible...Yeah, Right.

Okay, I get it. Each of us comes down on one side or the other of the fence on this one. So I'll qualify this, in hopes of getting you on my side of the fence. When I say "anything," I mean somewhat reasonable things. Things grounded in truth. So sure, you can tell me that it's not possible to snow in the desert in July, and I won't debate you. Let's stick with more realistic hopes and dreams. So if you want to be a rocket scientist, and you're thirty-two years old without a college degree, you can certainly do that. Or if you want to complete a triathlon and you don't know how to swim, or have only one foot, or weigh four hundred pounds…that goal is definitely possible. It might not be easy, but with the right mindset, it is possible.

In your organization, maybe you want to create a team who will respect each other and work collaboratively, though they are now acting passive-aggressive and undermining each other. Maybe you want to increase fundraising results by 50 percent, but donations have been trending in the other direction. Maybe you need to expand the board and form new committees in three months, but no one else seems to understand why. This, too, is all possible.

Just think…if nearly any goal or dream is possible, then imagine what we can accomplish! Take a minute and think about that one thing you've always wanted to do but haven't done yet. Maybe you don't know where to start, or how to line up the resources needed. Or maybe you have to admit that you just haven't believed it was possible until now. It's tickling the back of your brain, isn't it? You know why? Because it *is* possible. You can do it. Half the battle is truly wanting to do it—and since it's tickling you, that means you really do. Your heart may beat just a bit faster, and you may start to feel excited and a little nervous. Keep riding that feeling…stay with it. Your body is saying, *let's go!* So get out of the way and go with it.

The psychology behind all this is fascinating. I'm not a psychologist, but I know from experience that one of the most common reasons we don't go after our dreams is because we're afraid. We are afraid of failing, and sometimes of succeeding. Don't be a statistic. Focus. See that goal clearly. Now start believing you can reach it…believe beyond reason and beyond what may seem rational. Has anyone else ever done it? It's likely you'll be able to say yes and point to someone else who has achieved the same or a similar goal. So you *know* it's possible! And if no one else has had the same dream yet, how exciting to be the first!

Stop treading water. If you aren't confident quite yet, at least be curious. An executive director emailed me today saying how grateful she is for the opportunity to learn—nice! She is ready; she has the right mindset. She doesn't yet know how to make things happen, but she is ready and curious. Believe in your capacity to learn. Besides, if you aren't a little nervous, how can you commit? Doing the same old thing isn't motivating. So find new energy around what is important to you and the organization, and get unstuck. You are no longer a victim of your own brain; put the Impact Triangle to work and think about your mindset.

How to Start the Shift

What was true for Olympian Marilyn King is true for each of us in the nonprofit business as well. At www.freedictionary.com, *mindset* is defined as "n. 1. A fixed mental attitude or disposition that predetermines a person's responses to and interpretations of situations." We are talking about more than a positive attitude, or optimism. Those attitudes are related, but this dictionary definition is more powerful—your mindset is a *fixed* outlook, and therefore your behavior is *predetermined*. This type of perspective becomes ingrained so that in most situations in life, you look at things through this lens and believe in the importance of marching forward. Wow! Wouldn't it be great to maintain a winning mindset?

Sometimes believing in yourself takes guts. Most successful people started right where you may be now. They were attempting something they had never done before, but something kept them going forward. It was very important to them to be successful at achieving the goal. So they asked for help, conducted research, or did whatever it took to figure out what to try first. And by the way, there will be mistakes, and bumps along the way. So where do you start?

▶ Take a step back and assess your readiness to move forward. You can be surrounded by all the right people and have all the tools you need, but if you aren't prepared mentally for the ride, the odds of being successful are slim. Ask yourself, what is the worst thing that can happen if you fail? What if your team isn't on board? What needs to happen first to prepare for these types of scenarios? Where am I feeling vulnerable? Being self-aware in this way is a more advanced skill you can learn.

▶ Recruiting a support partner can be a big move toward success. Select a trustworthy friend, colleague, family member, or whomever you feel comfortable sharing your big goal with, and tell that person your plans. Do a quick check to be sure you consider this person to have a generally positive outlook; you don't want a negative knucklehead holding you back. Ask your partner to support you along the way by asking about progress periodically, encouraging you to stay focused on the big picture, reminding you to be flexible with benchmarks, and being a sounding board. Be sure to let him or her know what would be helpful to you. It's great to have an objective person to celebrate with or vent to, depending on the situation.

► The ability to maintain a big-picture perspective can be the difference between success and failure. Understanding the overarching end goal and remembering to refocus on it periodically will drive your behavior. It is easy to get distracted by the things that aren't going well or the things that are easiest for us to achieve. And every now and then, we all need some distraction. But when you find yourself adrift, overwhelmed, or lacking confidence to move forward, stop for a minute, take a breath, and look at the big picture. Focus on the amazing benefits of the end goal, remember that you only need to take the next step, and relax until you can reach a calmer state.

► We control how we choose to respond to situations in our life, so focus forward. I realize life isn't all rainbows and puppy dogs. So if a project is getting away from you, if a co-worker is slacking, or if the fundraiser is next week and you don't have anyone on the committee, you have a choice. Mope around, feel sorry for yourself, and drag down those around you, or stand up straight and figure out the next move.

► There can be no regrets. Several years ago at a Y staff retreat, we were introduced to the concept of being a Totally Responsible Person (TRP). This is a trademarked program and it really resonated with me. I have never been one to tolerate a victim mentality, or the need to blame, in people. It's not about judging them—I just don't get it. There will always be factors out of your control, but you get to define your own success. I believe if you're going to sit around and whine and complain, then that is what you will get in return—negative results. Conversely, if you look for a positive solution, focus on what can be learned, and believe that perseverance pays off, then odds increase that you will find yourself in a happier zone.

- Remember that you will need to direct your thinking. You may find it helpful to give yourself pep talks and create key phrases or mantras that work for you when they are repeated each day. Very simply stating that you are happy or excited about the possibilities can make a difference. If you are taking on a fundraising project, just for kicks, go crazy and tell yourself you are an expert fundraiser specializing in major gifts! Stick with it and see what happens as you move forward with the plan.
- Always remember to acknowledge progress. I can be so focused on the work, I sometimes forget to stop and do a little happy dance. You may need to actually calendar a progress review, to look back and review the past week, for instance. Take pride in both the big and little steps you are making. It really does feel good, and it inspires you to continue believing the end goal is achievable. You are creating possibility.

Do you know the book *Oh, the Places You'll Go!* by Dr. Seuss? In it, Dr. Seuss talks about the ups and downs of making one's life. My favorite part is:

> "You have brains in your head.
> You have feet in your shoes.
> You can steer yourself
> Any direction you choose.
> You're on your own. And you know what you know.
> And YOU are the guy who'll decide where to go."

Adjust your mindset and be responsible for our own success, however you define it. Go do the next great thing you were put on this earth to do. You are unstoppable, and you are equipped to take the next step of the Impact Triangle with me.

CHAPTER FOUR

RELATIONSHIPS MATTER

REMEMBER WHEN I WAS standing alone after the ground-breaking event? Clearly, I had overlooked the power of relationships. Things became so different once I realized that engaging people around things that matter to them is an important component of the Impact Triangle.

I was really blown away l when I decided to change professions. I had long served as an executive director for YMCAs, and decided to start a consulting company after several years of debate. During this transition, I reached out to people I knew to gain insight, get advice, and ask for introductions to others. No one turned me down, and over the course of four months, I had completed sixty-two informational interviews. I couldn't believe it—at first, I couldn't believe that the people I knew were so helpful. Then I was amazed at how many people they introduced me to who actually agreed to meet with me. Other connections were made through cold calls to people I found online that lived in other states, and *they* scheduled calls with me too. Just to be clear, these were executive directors of nonprofit organizations or leaders of companies and at universities; they were other busy consultants who shared how they got started; they were board members, and folks with an incredible amount of responsibility and influence.

I finally started asking the people I knew why they were so enthusiastically willing to help me (there's that curiosity thing). The responses all related to the same thing: I deserved it; I cared about them, or something they cared about all these years; they believed in me and wanted to see me be successful; I was clear about why I wanted to meet and respected their time. In other words, I had built up relationship capital.

I had learned over time that nurturing relationships and genuinely engaging people is powerful stuff. But the thing that really impressed me was how the people who *didn't* know me were also happy to help. And yes, they agreed to help because they respected the person who asked them. But there were also times when there was no connection—those cold calls to online sources—and they also spoke with me. It was craziness, I tell you! I kept looking around to see if I was being followed by a television crew who would tell me I was being punked. I slowly started to realize that in addition to benefitting from strong relationships, people are simply generous. Many of them also remembered people who had helped them along the way and contributed to their success. They continued to pay it forward.

People Are Generous

People will help you. They will get satisfaction just from being a tiny part of your success. This I know because I have been the fortunate recipient of much generosity in terms of advice, support, connections, leads, constructive criticism, and warm camaraderie. This fundamental belief about generosity and how we nurture our relationships is a primary premise of this book, and the foundation for so many successes. I have always felt fortunate to be surrounded by gracious, caring people who want to support others. Now, this isn't about being popular; it is about understanding that people care about you and will help you without asking for much, or anything, in return. Your network can also help you cope when things go sideways, and point out opportunities or different strategies.

If you start to take notice, you will see that people will step up to the plate when there is a need. There are many examples—when a natural disaster occurs, watch the donations pour in; when a neighbor experiences a death in the family, others move in with support; when a friend loses a job, people pull together and rally to gather resources. We are a compassionate lot, and I am here to say it is very rewarding to be on the receiving end of the generosity of many.

Most of us, especially if working in an organization focused on social impact, interact with many people every day. We communicate with vendors, volunteers, members, staff, colleagues, community partners, donors, and more. It can be tough to find time to keep up with basic communication, let alone have time to get strategic about true engagement. There are project deadlines, plans to implement, stories to tell, newsletters to post, budgets to monitor, and problems to solve. Very true… but you don't operate in a vacuum. The people alongside you are there to help you, too. Keep in mind, they are generous and they want to support you.

So how do we make this work?

- ▶ Identify those people who are strategically the most important to connect with first. Call it your Fabulous Fifty list, or perhaps your Terrific Twenty. They may be critical connections for various reasons. A city official who was instrumental in helping you secure land, a key donor who is well connected, a program participant with amazing loyalty—all these are examples of people you may want to know better for different reasons.
- ▶ Make time for strategic decisions around engagement, which is a systematic approach to deepening relationships. The benefits of cultivation are mutual to both people and can have a long-term effect. Employees reach a higher level of satisfaction and retention improves. Vendors will look for flexibility in negotiating contracts with you. Donors appreciate the sincere stewardship and will renew or increase their gifts. Volunteers will notice the recognition and step up to the plate on the next project.
- ▶ Be resourceful, and always be willing to reach out and ask—for advice, ideas, help, connections, and more. I'm willing to bet that if you are genuinely respectful and have solid values that make you credible, you will receive an astonishing amount of support. And be ready to be challenged—the best supporters will tell you what you don't want to hear, also.

► Staff, volunteers, vendors, donors, and colleagues expect us to hold them accountable as part of the team. It's true. What's the point of investing resources into a project if we aren't measuring success? We tend to do fairly well at this when it comes to monitoring staff performance. Beyond that, we get nervous. I'm here to tell you that you will gain more respect, and have more valuable and deeper relationships, when you realize that even volunteers want to be held accountable. And with stronger relationships come better performance, intrinsic motivation, and increased retention of donors, employees, and volunteers.

At the last YMCA where I worked, I frequently said, and honestly believed, that our board was made up of the most incredible volunteers. I realize it was because they believed in the mission, had clarity about their role and expectations, and focused on critical strategies to improve the community. I devoted much of my time to cultivating those relationships. I was committed to developing these people as leaders, providing meaningful experiences, and acknowledging them for the great work they did. At times it was difficult because of the dynamic nature of relationships. But as I look back, it was the natural course to take, and it was a fun endeavor from which I made lifelong friends.

And when asked why they stayed on the board, many volunteers cite that the relationships they made and the people they met were key factors. So if the social aspect of volunteering is mutually beneficial to staff and board members, why don't we put more effort and resources into cultivation and engagement strategies? I think we simply don't understand the remarkable potential behind these relationships.

One of the most common complaints of nonprofit executive directors is that the board isn't showing up—participation is low and they aren't meeting expectations. One of my first questions is, "What have you done in the last six months to engage them?" And the reality is that I either get a shoulder shrug or blank stare, or sometimes a report on weak attempts at engagement. The point is that once we understand what our volunteers need, we can go about learning how to provide it. We need them desperately, and a poorly performing, disengaged board can ruin an organization. If this is an issue for your organization, whether you are a board member or staff, then get moving and change the status quo.

Researchers at Booz Allen Hamilton and Northwestern University's Kellogg School, in a study of Fortune 1000 companies, found that the most successful and winning companies, the top 25 percent, all define and deploy relationships in a consistent, specific manner. In short, the most financially successful organizations are relationship focused. That's their differentiator.

People with the most social capital:
- Close deals faster
- Are more productive
- Receive larger bonuses
- Receive higher performance evaluations
  (*Forbes*, October 2010)

Keep in mind that this isn't a one-way street. When applying the Impact Triangle, share your valuable gifts with others, too. Then people will want to engage with you and create success together. This is related to the "rising tide raises all boats" concept—together we make extraordinary things happen.

CHAPTER FIVE

YOUR TOOLKIT

HAVE YOU EVER THOUGHT, "I have a clear fundraising goal, and a solid team who is inspired, but I don't know how to actually find people to ask for money, or even how to ask them"? Or maybe the question is about how to engage the board. There are many possible scenarios, and the point is that you want to find the best solutions for your business that lead the way to results. The right tools are a key component of the Impact Triangle and will take you across the finish line.

Here are some examples of the tools you need:

▶ **Strategy.** When you start on a project, identify the overarching direction or philosophy that will guide decisions. This will keep you from going in circles aimlessly.

▶ **Systems.** Create processes for projects, especially those that will be repeated. A step-by-step, sequential procedure adds clarity and direction.

▶ **Templates.** A good system will incorporate templates and forms that can be customized. You certainly don't want to re-create a good product each time you need it.

▶ **Team.** It will serve you well to have the right people in the right places at the right time to get things done right.

- **Training and development.** Invest in people. Invest in everyone's growth, and definitely remember those who will deliver the programs and services. It will directly affect your organization's impact.
- **Resources.** Know where you can find examples of winning practices. Who are the experts, what are the best publications, how can you research the latest trends, what are great questions to ask?
- **Technology.** Try to understand how the remarkable advancements in this digital age can support your efforts. You cannot be hesitant here, or your organization will become irrelevant.
- **Evaluation.** Always, always establish methods to review and assess your work. There are several ways to do so, and you will grow faster and accelerate your impact when you value this process.

At different times, depending on the project and your role, you will need different tools. It is best to identify which ones are necessary early on and strive to line them up in advance. When I was standing alone after the ground-breaking event that day, I had a pretty strong collection of tools. I had planned well, had managed the logistical details, and had an overall strategy for a successful event. During preparation, it had felt great to check off all the boxes on my list. But, as is so commonly the case, the rest of my Impact Triangle was a mess.

The lesson for us in the nonprofit business is to understand that all three parts of the Impact Triangle are necessary in order to be successful. Choose to be responsible for your future. By doing things differently, even though it may be a challenge, you can expect different results. You can expect to stop the chaos and stress, and thrive.

CHAPTER SIX

CHANGE WILL BE REQUIRED

YOU HAVE PROBABLY PICKED up on a theme by now—in order to achieve significant impact in the community, this new approach involves some type of change. It could be gaining a new perspective, approaching a relationship differently, creating a new process or system, organizing differently, etc. And almost anytime there is change, there is likely to be tension, fear, and frustration. It is a time of uncertainty, perhaps instability, and there is questioning as well as some degree of resistance. A good deal of thought and planning is required to manage this well. The good news is that this craziness is normal and necessary to get to extraordinary results.

Recently, I was working with an organization to develop a more structured recruiting and engagement process in order to strengthen their board. It was exciting and fun for me, because they were ready. And yet, as the shift in culture started to unfold, the grumpy faces and challenging remarks came out, too. I was prepared for some of this, but it still wasn't easy. I asked for members' input and feedback to make sure their mark was on the plan. I strived to keep them focused on the "why," the big picture. From the beginning, I let them know there would be times when it would feel like they were taking one step forward and two steps back. These things take time, but the goal is to keep moving forward.

Then one day, the grumpiest guy had a breakthrough—he realized his desire to help the organization far exceeded his desire to be stubborn and anxious about a new way of doing things. He uncrossed his arms and started to fully participate; he offered to introduce a key player to the organization, and the ball was rolling! Others responded favorably and the energy was palpable. When you come out on the other side of change, it can be very rewarding. Looking back, those board members said it was a good process that helped them bond as a team and engage on a deeper level individually. Mission accomplished.

There is a book by William Bridges, PhD, called *Managing Transitions: Making the Most of Change*. It focuses a lot on the psychology of what he deems to be a three-stage process: the end zone (letting go of something), the neutral zone (transition), and the new beginning. In the example above, the board had to let go of what they were doing—a lackadaisical, shot-in-the-dark style of recruiting with a weak orientation system—and adopt a more engaged, deliberate process that targeted people who could bring specific talent to advance their mission. It's harder work. But as Bridges points out, if you manage the transition well, chances are better the team will move along with the plan and feel satisfied with the end results.

Consider these tips when change is on the horizon:

▸ **Ensure alignment with mission and values.** Sometimes we get excited about a new idea that just sounds great! We rush to bring others on board, and then realize it's not consistent with the values of the organization. Or it's contributing to mission creep, expanding a project beyond the original purpose. An important first step in introducing a change is testing it against your mission and values. For example, if your organization is committed to services that are self-sufficient or produce a certain margin, introducing a new program that loses money without any regard for a funding plan could be a major issue. There is certainly opportunity to welcome discussion around the point, but going blindly forward without testing the idea could be troublesome. To have the best chance of bringing others on board, you want to avoid a false start due to misalignment.

▸ **Expect resistance.** Sit back and think through what your expectations are for the "new thing." Maybe it is staff reorganization, a new database that will affect everyone's work, or perhaps a new facility that entails a big move. Whatever it is, think about how the people involved may feel. While you can't anticipate every response, it will be helpful to think the situation through in advance. Do they have a voice? Is it truly going to be harder on them, or just different? What will the benefits be when the change is complete? What's the effect on the organization? Who will be affected—staff, volunteers, vendors, donors, program participants, or others?

Think it through, put yourself in their shoes, and plan for the worst while hoping for the best. There's no reason it has to be a hot mess. It's easy to picture the positive results of the change, but you must think about the in-between period when the change is occurring, too—the transition. Try to plan, and also be aware of whatever unfolds so you can notice what emerges. You can likely manage much of the possible resistance.

▶ **Include others in the planning.** When you or someone on your team has identified a needed change, try to include others in the planning. If it's possible to include people at several levels, or in different roles, that could be helpful in managing the transition. If there are champions throughout the organization, people who can relate to what most others will go through, that's ideal.

However, it's possible to include too many people. When this happens, the process gets bogged down because everyone provides input on the plan. You are striving to find the balance. The point is that you will benefit from various perspectives and from understanding more clearly the issues that affect others; the other members of the team will feel valued because you chose to include them in this important work. There may not always be time to include all the people you would like, which is where the next tip comes into play.

▶ **Communicate like crazy.** Before, during, and after. A significant component of the plan is to determine how, when, what, and with whom will you communicate. Who needs to know what's coming? Should you communicate individually, or in groups? Will an email suffice, or should it be in person? And how frequently will there be updates and check-ins?

Being transparent builds trust. You're in a situation that increases anxiety and if you keep people in the dark, it will just get worse. The change must have *a clear purpose,* and the team needs to hear the "why" behind it. Share what you perceive the *benefits* of the change as being, as well as what you think *might be hard, different or complicated.* It won't be all rainbows and butterflies, so try not to overpromise on the positive outcomes.

▸ **Listen.** Yes, listening is part of communicating, but it's so important it gets its own bullet. When you let everyone know about this fabulous new change, don't miss the opportunity to listen to what is being said. Really listen. Ask open-ended questions to find out what people think about the plan, especially if there is a lot of silence—in this case, silence is generally not good. Try questions such as, "How are you feeling about the proposed new system?", "What else would be helpful for you to know?", "How do think we should be communicating the change?" and "Who do you think we should include in the planning?" You can learn a lot about what people are thinking if you just ask. And wouldn't it be nice if you could calm some of the fear and frustration early on by listening? You may learn that a slight adjustment in direction can alleviate many headaches for everyone down the road.

▸ **Keep moving forward.** Here's the thing…different people will react in different ways to change. Eventually most push through their trepidation, even if there is some initial resistance, which could manifest itself in a bad attitude, showing up late and leaving early, avoidance, or being disruptive. And while you will want to support and encourage folks throughout the process, at some point everyone needs to move forward. So don't get stuck. Not everyone will get on board and be pleased at the same time—keep moving the plan forward anyway. There will absolutely be bumps in the road.

If you believe in the process, have a good plan with a purpose, have included folks in the planning, and communicated well, problems will likely resolve themselves. Along the way, you may have to have a difficult conversation with some people who are dragging their feet. But you wouldn't be going through the change if you didn't think it was worth it. Direct the energy forward, focus on the big picture, and keep on moving.

▸ **Thank and celebrate.** I have to say, it is pretty cool when you make it through the transition, everyone has survived (or even if you lost one or two people along the way—it's sometimes better that way), and the team is moving forward with the new system, plan, program, building, or other change. Try to remember to celebrate the little wins, too, as you go along. When you see people put down their resistance and get aligned with the purpose, acknowledge that and thank them—it may have been tough for them to get to that place. And when you are through to the other side, certainly thank the team who stood beside you during the journey, who stepped up and were a part of the process. There are people who love change, but even they will tell you that at times it gets a bit overwhelming or nerve-wracking.

Change is happening all around you. Whether you initiate it or not, it's here to stay. Keep an open mind, consider what's possible, and really try to stay positive and flexible. Put the Impact Triangle to work by approaching change with an effective mindset, honor the people who are along for the ride, and utilize the tools that are most likely to guide you toward the most significant impact.

Summary of Key Points

1. The Impact Triangle focuses on the three proven ways to grow and increase the impact of your organization: adopt the right mindset and approach; engage in strategic relationships; and use the best practices and tools for your business.

2. The four areas that businesses with a social mission find most challenging are planning, building strong boards, fundraising, and staff management.

3. Nonprofit leaders need to change the story—to be proud of their thriving social impact businesses and perpetuate a positive image. It's time to stop thinking about scarcity and instead create abundance.

4. Successful nonprofit leaders approach their work differently than those who consistently struggle. They set goals that they are passionate about and believe they are possible to achieve.

5. A shift in mindset will determine behavior. To get started, try these steps: assess your readiness for a shift, recruit a support partner, maintain a big-picture perspective, focus forward, have no regrets, direct your thinking, and acknowledge progress.

6. Engaging people around things that matter to them is an important part of the Impact Triangle. People are generous and get satisfaction from being a part of success.

7. In order to strategically strengthen relationships, we must identify who is most important to connect with, make time for strategic decisions regarding engagement, be resourceful, and hold people accountable.

8. Successful engagement results in increased productivity, higher retention, and better performance of both staff and volunteers.

9. Some tools and best practices that you will need to increase impact include strategy, systems, templates, a strong team, training and development, resources, technology, and evaluation.

10. You will need different tools at different times, and you will have to customize them according to your organization's specific needs.

11. The Impact Triangle is a new approach and will require some change. Some tips for managing change include: ensure alignment with mission

and values, expect resistance, include others in the planning, communicate, listen, keep moving forward, thank, and celebrate.

Action Steps

1. Reflect on these things:
    - ► How do you present your organization when telling the story?
    - ► How can the Impact Triangle be most helpful to you?
    - ► Are you ready to make some changes?
2. Share your above reflections with a trusted colleague or friend, and determine what needs to happen next.

PART TWO

APPLYING THE IMPACT TRIANGLE TO PLANNING

2

CHAPTER SEVEN

THERE *IS* ENOUGH TIME

THIS COULD BE A TOUGH ONE, because you may disagree with me, so hang on. Many, if not all, of us have complained at some point that there simply is not enough time to do everything that needs to get done, especially when it comes to planning. There are many competing priorities and even more details to manage. Time is the number one or two obstacle nonprofit leaders identify. I get it, because I have felt the same way.

No one likes to be overworked; even the martyrs among us get burned out at some point. When work is overwhelming, it's stressful, and that takes a toll on our health. When we're stressed and not feeling great, we take longer to do things, and guess what? We don't have time to waste, so let's focus on working smart to make the most of our time.

And now I'm going to tell you there *is* enough time to plan. Do you know how I know this? Because there are people who are getting things done who have similar workloads, resources, and expectations to yours. They aren't smarter than you, nor do they have PhD's in super-efficiency and time management. Instead, they embraced the perspective of investing in some planning up front; of working smart to achieve the top priorities in their key areas of focus. They understand the Impact Triangle. As it turns out, it is the plan that directs our work and determines our priorities—not the clock.

An organization in Arizona with a wonderful mission, and highly regarded in the community, had operated very well for over two decades. They were well resourced, had strong leadership, and the operation was chugging along. Then the executive director retired, and some of the board members moved on, too. The newly established team, still comprised of very bright and capable people, continued to move the organization forward and serve more people. But one key ingredient was missing: they didn't establish a clear direction. The strategic plan was now six years old, and it became clear that what was working under the previous leadership team was no longer as effective. The board and staff were feeling more scattered and reactionary than ever before. Donations slowed, committee members no longer felt they were doing meaningful work, and staff morale fell.

About nine months into his tenure, the new executive director realized they needed to take time to regroup. He gathered the team of board and staff, and they reached a consensus that the main issue was lack of direction. Some of the former strategies were still relevant, but the new team, with new talent and ideas, needed to work together to establish clear goals that they owned and were excited to implement. The good news is that within eighteen months this organization was surpassing previous levels of success, with plans to build a new facility. The plan was directing the work because the new team had established clear priorities.

As you can see, the ability to see results in a reasonable period of time at work is not just about typical "time management" advice. Just search the internet and you'll find dozens of sites with great tips to improve your efficiency, such as:

- Make a weekly plan
- Avoid unnecessary distractions
- Say no to unnecessary tasks
- Delegate
- Keep a time log (this can be a real eye-opener!)
- Create an organizational system

These can all be important to managing time in general, and I recommend them. However, the real difference between people who can get the job done and those who complain about not enough time is their mindset. When you place high enough value on something, you will find the time to get it done. And a good plan will help you identify those priorities so you can focus your energy effectively.

When the work is important to the mission, start talking as though you believe it's possible to get tasks completed in a timely fashion without killing yourself. In other words, start believing it! Then take a few steps to change how you are working. Start by recognizing what might be blocking your success.

▶ Is it a people issue? Materials? Communication? Technical?

▶ Are you procrastinating because you need to have a difficult conversation?

▶ Is the "to be filed" pile over two feet tall and about to slip onto the floor any minute?

Look for the obstacle—and I mean, really look. You are not a victim here. Choose to look at it differently and invest time in the right places. Then you will start to feel that you have some control over the situation.

As with any change, you might feel a little uncomfortable. Most change requires us to let go of something...a way we've been doing something, a favorite system or tool, or perhaps a collegial relationship that may be altered if a new team member is part of the change. So don't ignore the emotional side of things. What you're feeling is normal and needs some air time. Acknowledge this, and accept the discomfort for a bit. Then focus forward.

The goal is to work smart—to focus on the action that will give you the greatest return and have the most impact. In other words, *prioritize your work with return on investment in mind.* This will actually save you time in the long run. Be careful to limit your top areas of focus, however. One mistake I see fairly often is having eight or more critical priorities. That won't work, because the priorities themselves become distractions. Really focus on only two or three; otherwise you will find yourself spinning your wheels in a vicious cycle. Take a step back and look at the big picture.

For example, if building a strong board is a key initiative in your strategic plan, it makes sense for this to be one of your critical areas of focus. And board development is complicated and takes time, which is affecting your mindset. But stay with me here.

- What if you shut your door, and determine what needs to get done in the next ninety days?
- Next, lay out a strategy for what needs to be complete in sixty days, and thirty days.
- How does that affect your weekly and daily actions?
- Then commit to doing just one thing (making a phone call, identifying who your champions are, drafting a timeline, etc.) related to the plan each day. Some days just reviewing the plan may be enough.

In this case, by investing time in the right place (planning), you can avoid a feeling of being overwhelmed and start to see how to break the project into manageable pieces.

Additionally, others will see your progress, and you will have more champions willing to step up and support your next project. Both the strategy creation and execution take time—and the benefit is significant, so it is a smart use of time. This is like doing a cost-benefit analysis—look at return on investment and your perspective will start to shift. Every step you take is a choice.

I do want to emphasize that I'm not suggesting you cut corners anywhere. Even when tasks are of less importance, they still deserve your full attention and commitment to quality. Rushing through things can result in needing to repeat the task, and then you're faced with an incredible time waster. We are trying to deposit more time in your account, not suck the life out of it.

Focus

Each person's method of working most effectively will vary, but one key ingredient to being successful is your ability to focus. Artists and athletes refer to being in "the zone." Same idea…laser-like focus is an absolute advantage to working smart.

- Environment becomes important when you attempt to zero in on the critical work you've outlined for yourself. Think of things like noise, email, access to others, comfort, etc. It may seem overly simple, but really take a look at your options. If you aren't working from home part of the time, consider it. Of course, if you have six kids at home, two dogs, and no quiet place, this may not be the answer. I had a colleague who would go to the neighborhood library every year around budget time. He loved it because he could whip out the laptop and go to town developing great budget plans, and no one could bug him. And do you know what he said? He got more done there in two hours than he would all day in the office.

▶ I also know a wonderful lady who felt it was unprofessional to put her phone on "do not disturb" or close her office door. I understood it was an individual preference and respected it, but I encouraged her to find ways to overcome the frustration of not having enough time. Finally, she got to the point where she would send out an email telling all key staff that she was going to close her door for the next hour and to please hold all inquiries until after that time. When the earth did not stop spinning, she realized it might be okay to do this occasionally.

▶ I, on the other hand, would work from home most mornings, close my door, use DND, have stand-up meetings, let folks know how long I could take for a discussion, and do whatever it took to get the critical work done. The trick is balancing that skill with being available to people when you need to be, so they don't perceive you as distant and uncaring.

▶ I also encourage you to remember why you are in this job in the first place. Okay—yes, you need to make a living, but besides the paycheck and the pats on the back you get from your supervisor, *why do you do this work?* Especially for people who work in organizations that focus on a social mission, the motivation typically comes from somewhere else. Your ability to impact the community, and perhaps the world, is profound. You get to inspire others every day. People look to you with respect and admiration as you go about your important work. What you do really matters, and you can change things for others. It seems to me that getting serious about how you approach this work is a small request.

A word about those things in our jobs we really don't like to do. We all have them, and usually there is no way around them. (I know because I once tried to delegate them all and it backfired!) So just suck it up. Play whatever game you need to, but get the tasks done. If you procrastinate too long, it just creates more stress, and you don't have time for that. Make a deal with yourself: for twenty minutes a day, or three times a week—whatever works best—just do the things you can't stand. Give it a name like TRS (This Really Sucks) time and just get on with it. We're adults, and life isn't fair sometimes.

► Finally, keep this in mind: in order to be your best, you must take care of yourself. Working long hours isn't healthy, and trust me—even if you don't think so, you're bringing less than your best to others also. Remember me and the lonely post-ground-breaking example.

Take breaks throughout the day and walk around, or go outside and clear your head. Speaking of breaks, schedule your vacations for the next year. Really. Pull out that calendar…look for opportunities to take some long weekends; visit friends you haven't seen in a long time; go lie on a beach, or ski that mountain you never visited; drive up the coast, or out in the countryside; chaperone your child's class trip, take a painting class, ride on a train, or canoe the lake. It doesn't matter what it is, but disconnect from work! Working smart also means recognizing that working all the time is dumb. Seriously, you are not that important. No offense, but even the President of the United States takes vacations.

Get enough sleep, eat well, and don't use the excuse of not having enough time to cook as a reason to fill yourself with junk. Respect yourself more than that—you deserve it. And while I am a near fanatic about the importance of exercise, I will simply say that in addition to the health benefits, some level of physical activity most days of the week will actually result in getting your work done in less time. When you feel better, you have more energy and a more positive outlook, and you are open to what is possible. Finally, whether at home or work, when you're tired or distracted, it negatively affects your relationships. And we know how important it is to be nurturing in your relationships (see chapter 4). Investing in your health means investing in all other aspects of your life, too.

When you shift your perspective to invest in planning, to work smart, and to stay mentally sharp, you will start to see changes in the progress you can make on your key initiatives. The Impact Triangle will play a major role in helping you make this shift.

CHAPTER EIGHT

STRATEGIC VERSUS TACTICAL

OKAY, I KNOW. This is the part of the book you want to skip. Try not to roll your eyes and become comatose. You want to achieve excellence, and setting a strategic direction is necessary. Please indulge me for just a bit, and let's see if we can get you to change your perspective. After all, we know mindset matters.

We tend to think of planning in general, and strategic planning especially, as a distraction that takes us away from our work, when actually, it is the plan that directs our work and determines our priorities. When we focus on the plan, we can be highly productive; without it, achieving success is much more challenging. Without a plan, how do you know where you're going?

Now, I don't happen to think strategic planning needs to take many months to get right, though some of my colleagues will disagree. There are critical components of the plan that require due diligence, but let's make the process as simple as we can, because you don't have the luxury of extra time.

First, let's get clear on what strategic planning is:

- *Strategy* refers to planning your next moves for the organization.
- It's future-oriented and involves making decisions about the direction of the company.

- It outlines what will get done, why, when, and by whom.
- The emphasis is on the big picture and long-term goals, usually in three-to-five-year increments.
- Typically the strategic plan is created by the board and upper management.

It's not unusual for folks to get excited about the plan and start moving into discussions about tactics. Here is the difference:

- *Tactic* refers to how the plan will be implemented.
- It is based on the present—the current state of things.
- The emphasis is shorter term, typically the current year.
- Many people at all levels of the organization may be involved in execution of the plan.

Try to keep this distinction clear, and focus on strategy when looking forward at high-level issues. Then switch to tactics when outlining how to accomplish the areas of focus, and start with the present time. As a leader in an organization, whether a staff or board member, you need to think both strategically and tactically. You could have a great vision, but without specific action plans, you won't achieve goals. And if there is no strategic direction, you can be very busy doing a lot of unnecessary things that also keep you from being successful. If you are still unsure why planning strategically should be a high priority, check out the results of this study.

Executive Summary:

The Association for Strategic Planning (ASP) conducted a national survey in March 2012 regarding successful practices in strategic planning for nonprofit 501(c)(3) organizations. Initial findings of the 1,000+ responses revealed the following three items of significant interest:

1. The driver for strategic planning in high-success organizations is "Routine periodic process in our organization."

    Whereas in low-success organizations, the driver for planning is "Driven by significant risks/challenges."

2. Successful organizations report having successful plan implementation practices; low-success organizations report that they do not have successful implementation practices.

3. Highly successful organizations report that strategic planning has high impact on overall organizational success.

   Low-success organizations do not report strategic planning as key to overall organizational success

   (You can find more information at their site www.strategyplus.org)

In other words, the most successful organizations have made strategic planning part of their culture, they have systems for implementation, and this has had a positive impact on their success. So I hope you're on board, and ready to embrace the need to set strategic direction. You may not know how, but we'll outline a few tips here, and then it's just about being committed enough to take the first step.

Process

1. I believe the strategic planning process should be a *group dynamic* involving staff and board members. It is a wonderful engagement strategy— when people are involved in setting the direction of your organization, it helps them get excited about having a sense of ownership and pride in being part of the leadership team. They are also more likely to feel committed to the implementation of the plan. Allowing staff and volunteers to identify big issues and analyze the whole environment in which the organization operates can truly motivate them.

2. I also agree with the philosophy that *key stakeholders should get involved* in the strategic planning process. Board members, staff leadership, key donors, influential partners, and perhaps even beneficiaries can shed valuable light on this work. Many perspectives ensure there are no blind spots—diversity drives innovation.

   If this idea is making you squirm a bit, stop and ask why. It's not unusual to feel that this should be a closed-door discussion, as you analyze and brainstorm your most critical practices and ideas. But if you have some additional people in the room for the process who really care about the business, chances are your plan will be even stronger and right on track. And keep the Impact Triangle in mind—deepening relationships is essential to your success. How much fun would it be to invite the superintendent of schools, the police chief, the president of the Chamber of Commerce, the Recreation Department director, the head of the Farmers Association, and several others to discuss major issues and trends facing the community? This could be a great springboard to thoughtful discussion.

3. I am a proponent of utilizing an *outside facilitator* to run your planning process, for two reasons: an expert who does this regularly will bring a high level of professionalism and strong guidance, and this person also will be objective. It's not the facilitator's plan, whereas if a board member or CEO facilitates, it's very hard for that person to stay objective. I had a board member who is a master facilitator in planning tell me she really wanted to participate as a board member, and not miss out on the process because she was in the facilitator role. I thought that was an excellent point. So this is a good time to leverage your relationships and call on people you know who may be in the field, or someone who could recommend a strong facilitator.

4. There are *different methodologies* that can get the same result, and when it comes to planning, several are good. David La Piana is an expert at strategic planning and has a great book called *The Nonprofit Strategy Revolution.* He outlines these three elements as basic to successful strategy:

    ► A sound business model (who you are, what you do, how you do it, and how it's financed)
    ► Market awareness (what your market is, where you are in it, how you got there, and where to go next)
    ► Competitive advantage (unique assets or outstanding execution)

5. You will notice that a solid process *will look both internally at the organization and outwardly* to analyze those factors in the external environment that could affect business. So in addition to assessing your services, finances, etc., you will identify trends, emerging markets, demographic shifts, and other relevant data in the community you serve. All of this information will assist you in identifying what the strengths of the organization are, where there may be risk, and future opportunities that are well matched to your mission. A traditional SWOT or SOAR analysis can be utilized, and I think it's worth looking at alternatives to traditional planning sessions. La Piana is a great resource for fresh ideas on how to get to the same result in less time with somewhat more straightforward activities.

   You may be wondering where you get the external data in the first place. Each community is different, but typically there are already studies and sources out there to tap into, such as city governments, school districts, foundations, health and human service organizations, economic development corporations, and of course the internet. There is a fair amount of up-front work that staff will need to complete before the conversations really begin. You will gather this information and then roll it up into a format that is easy to interpret and focuses on key data points.

   To ensure you are going to meet expectations, I would recommend having a discussion at a board meeting or with key leaders to determine what information is needed in order to effectively analyze both internal and external environments. And a word of caution: you can gather too much data. I have seen processes that got bogged down in reams of reports. Zero in on what you really need to know. While you need some facts, many times some good intuition and basic knowledge will fill in the gaps.

6. I have learned that the ability to *ask the right questions* during this process is an art—and the effect can be significant. Otherwise, you can slog through the process without any provocative discussion, and not only is that no fun, but you could end up with a generic plan that lacks inspiration and may not reach toward real opportunity. Questions you could ask include:

- ▶ What could we do better than anyone else?
- ▶ How can we generate revenue differently?
- ▶ What services should we cease because they are no longer relevant?

So when you frame the work with your facilitator, be sure to ask how that person will utilize questions as a way to get at the heart of issues, both positive and otherwise.

Once the planning committee has completed the process, it will be recommended to the board for approval. If progress on the planning has been regularly communicated, and all volunteers have had a chance to participate, this part of the process typically flows pretty smoothly. Send a draft of the plan in advance so board members can review it, which will allow for more meaningful discussion in a board meeting.

Components

All plans have some key components that are essential for them to be effective. Once you have gathered the collective wisdom of your key stakeholders, and have settled in on some key focus areas, it's time to organize the discussion in writing. I am a firm believer that you can have too many goals—a plan that has three to four major initiatives for the next three to five years works best, from my perspective. I worked with an organization that selected eight major goals, and they ended up working in circles because one goal served as a distraction for another. So try this:

- ▶ Three to four major focus areas
- ▶ Several strategies for each focus area
- ▶ Success measures and intended impact
- ▶ Action steps/tactics
- ▶ Clear timeline
- ▶ Resources outlined
- ▶ Plan for monitoring and communicating back to stakeholders

As I've said before, an outline of key focus areas and strategies for achieving your goals is what drives you toward success. It's also essential to understand that *being adaptive and nimble is a success strategy*. So while the plan is in place, and you are working toward implementation, build in those systems for assessment and adaptation. Intentionally keep an eye on trends that may crop up unexpectedly. Our world changes faster than ever, and being aware of these factors will help you stay focused forward, navigating the best course for advancing your mission. For you type A's out there, don't be afraid to be flexible; it doesn't mean you're cheating when you adjust course.

CHAPTER NINE

THE ACCOUNTABILITY OF EXECUTION

EXECUTING THE PLAN IS NOT as hard as you may think. So direct your thinking differently, and go all in. After all that you have invested in developing the right mindset, pulling the team together, focusing on key strategies, and knowing it is able to be accomplished, you don't want to just put the plan away without seeing it come to fruition. As a matter of fact, I believe a critical step in the planning process, while the team is all together, is to agree on how the plan will be executed and decide what support structures need to be in place to ensure success. This is applicable for a budget plan, program plan, strategic plan, facility plan, marketing plan, etc.

So what are your options to hold yourself and your team accountable for execution of your plan? It seems to me that every road you choose needs to be comfortable for those who are accountable. So the executive director and key board members might want to have the most to say about methodology.

Remember...you can expect what you inspect. What gets measured gets done. It is important to establish *meaningful* success measures that are aligned with the key strategies. At the end of the day you are most interested in the social impact your organization is having on the community. That can be measured in many ways and I really like this website for a lesson in measurement:

www.staceybarr.com "The Performance Measure Specialist." There are free resources available on the site too.

Here are a few thoughts on how to operationalize a plan, and you can mix and match to fit your culture.

Dashboards

I'm a big fan. But only if they are one page and are truly a summary of key success indicators, with a timeline and accountability function. In other words, if the dashboard goes into too much detail about why, and demographics and such, it basically looks like the original plan and doesn't provide focus or simplicity. Or if it's measuring the wrong things, it won't be relevant.

An effective dashboard will list the key initiatives, the expected time frame, and who is being held accountable to get everything done. And if it is color coded with green, yellow, and red—yahoo! Now you really have people's attention and you can generate some energy around it.

Keep in mind that the main reason a plan doesn't get executed is because people aren't sure where to start, and it seems overwhelming. A dashboard allows you to break a comprehensive plan into smaller sections that aren't so intimidating. One page with groovy colors seems much more achievable, and we know it's very important to be able to believe it can be done.

Communication

You want to be sure the plan and the progress toward goals aren't kept a secret. So who needs to be kept in the loop? Depending on the type of plan, it may be prudent to keep most groups affiliated with the organization informed. That includes staff, board members, donors, participants, beneficiaries, vendors, volunteers, members, etc. If it's an operational budget plan, perhaps only staff and board members will be regularly updated. But I would caution you to keep your participants and donors informed on any key points that could affect their experience with the organization. For instance, if you have decided to reduce services to an area because the need has decreased, be up front about it so you are perceived as being transparent. So how do we do this effectively?

Utilize systems that are already in place as much as you can. If you have a weekly email blast that goes out to staff, include the goals or progress there. You could even paste the dashboard, or relevant sections, right in the email. Think about how you could use your website to announce movement toward goals. And what about meetings? For a strategic plan, I think you have missed the mark if it isn't discussed at board meetings about every quarter. The goal is to keep attention on the critical areas of focus so each board member knows what his or her role is to ensure implementation. For example, if there is a need to enhance marketing efforts, then the volunteers on the committee that was tasked with overseeing this work would report to the rest of the board four times a year. This will inherently increase accountability, which moves the plan forward.

Review other methods of communication you now have in place. Perhaps you can roll out a major plan at an all-staff meeting. An annual report is a nice way to show key initiatives and progress made as well as future plans. And who knows—a key donor could step up to support the effort, or maybe you can iden-tify a board prospect who is interested in seeing that things get accomplished.

The good news about having a social mission is that people in the commu-nity really care about what you're doing, because they will likely be impacted. Communication deepens commitment, so let's share success stories and announce future plans! To that end, why not get on the meeting agendas of community groups and service clubs? What a great way to get the word out, and get valuable feedback while cultivating some relationships! And once the general community knows what you are up to, there will be additional motivation to keep your nose to the grindstone.

Adapt

If you haven't experienced this yet, let me be the first to assure you that despite your best efforts, things will not go exactly according to plan. The timing may be a bit off. There could be outside factors, beyond your control, that significantly impact the plan.

In 2001, California experienced an energy crisis resulting in a major utility rate increase. It suddenly became clear that our YMCA budget plan was no longer realistic. After considerable research and careful thought, we decided to add a utility surcharge fee onto our Y membership rates. It wasn't very popular, but we determined the choice was to either cut services or pass along some costs. We were careful to communicate well, and when things smoothed out, we dropped the surcharge. Our members stayed loyal because we worked hard to build trust and remain transparent.

So I suggest that during the planning process, you discuss the need to be flexible. Some things won't be negotiable. But many can be—whether it's the calendar, or a third of the way through a project you realize the benchmark for success was set too low, or additional assessments indicate a certain priority has dropped from urgent to a lower status. Understanding that it's acceptable to revisit and adjust along the way can be very reassuring.

And try to remember to keep an eye on the people around you. Some may start to doubt the plan because implementation is difficult. You may need to try to inspire (or ignore?) those doubters. It may indeed get hard, but change can take time, and when the impact is critical it's important to be patient. The present is only temporary, so look for ways to infuse energy into positive movement forward. Go to your champions when you feel drained yourself—it takes a village, and there is power in your relationships.

Resources

Sometimes a plan never gets executed because the necessary resources aren't lined up sufficiently. It is the board's responsibility to see that the organization is well resourced and the executive director's responsibility to see that resources are allocated to support the plan. It's also important to assess systems and procedures to ensure any obstacles are removed. In the meantime, I say let's stop playing the victim. There will never be enough resources, meaning you can always utilize more.

Focus on what you can do to improve the situation, and get done what you can for now. Things will evolve as momentum is gained. People want to be a part of a winning initiative, so get started anyway. I recognize that it may be difficult to not get immediate gratification. But you will start to get traction in the short run, and eventually you'll see the desired results looming large.

So continue to believe, and call on those around you so their collective wisdom will help you gather the resources needed to make progress. You don't have to have it figured out all at once. For such a young guy, I think Robert Griffin III is very smart. As he was accepting his NFL Offensive Rookie of the Year award, he said, "It's not always what you get for the team, it's what you're willing to give for the team." When you give it all you can, you will be moving forward toward the goal, even if all your ducks aren't lined up in a row.

Mary Andrews, business and life coach, introduced me to a great tool to support execution—a *milestone chart*. I call it "sliding in backwards." In other words, determine when you need to hit the end goal. If it's eight months from now, where do you have to be in six months, four months, two months, and what needs to happen this month, and this week? By setting up this type of milestone chart, the work feels manageable. You can use these benchmarks with staff and volunteers to create team energy.

For example, if you need to recruit forty campaigners in four months, that's ten per month; which means you need to have fifteen meetings per month, assuming one-third will decline the invitation. So that means three to four meetings a week need to be scheduled by the team to ensure success. I don't know about you, but to me that seems less daunting than "I need to recruit forty campaigners!"

Performance Monitoring

Most organizations form an ad hoc strategic planning committee or utilize an existing one, perhaps the Executive committee. This committee will facilitate the planning process, and when it's complete they will either monitor execution or hand off responsibility to a standing committee that is accountable for overseeing the long-term implementation.

Both staff and board members are ultimately accountable for the execution of a strategic plan; staff are the primary implementers of operational plans, such as the budget. At times, adjustments in expectations may need to be made to manage gaps in performance toward reaching goals. In addition to dashboards, which summarize progress toward goals, tools for measuring people's performance should be optimized also.

Most organizations utilize some type of staff performance standards for evaluation purposes. These standards will need to be aligned with the goals of the organization. Job descriptions are based on these priorities. The annual work plans for committees will also reflect the key strategy areas for the organization. When each team is clearly working toward the same goal, much can be achieved.

Successful organizations perform annual board evaluations, and metrics relate to whether the annual goals were achieved. Such an evaluation asks about the degree to which key initiatives were met, and the board development committee can analyze results and measure success. These organizations will then adjust as needed by focusing more resources in areas that may be falling short and strengthening strategies around the areas that are reaping the most benefit. The key is that someone, somewhere, needs to be monitoring progress regularly and reporting back to leadership.

Accountability ends up being a natural part of the planning process when it is clear who is responsible for the goals and systems are established to measure progress. Your team invested in this important process and will be energized by progress. This best practice of assessment is a critical tool and part of the Impact Triangle.

Summary of Key Points

1. Planning directs your work and determines your priorities; it is not a distraction from your work.

2. Time management is only part of the equation when trying to find time to plan. When you place high enough value on something, you will find the time to get it done.

3. A key ingredient to success is the ability to focus; environment is critical.

4. Plan to support your health, get enough sleep, and take vacations; the healthier you are, the more valuable and capable you are to the organization.

5. Strategic planning is formulating a plan for your organization's next moves. It is future-oriented and involves making decisions about the direction of the company. It includes an outline of what will get done, why, when, and by whom. It emphasizes the big picture and long-term goals, usually in three-to-five-year increments. It is created by the board and upper management.

6. A tactical approach is the way the plan will be implemented, based on the present. It emphasizes a shorter term, typically the current year, and involves many people at all levels of the organization in execution of the plan.

7. Successful planners will involve key stakeholders, use an outside facilitator, adopt a proven process through which critical questions about both internal and external environments are posed, and realize the plan is a framework to be adapted appropriately.

8. Components of a strategic plan include:
    Three to four major focus areas
    Several strategies for each focus area
    Success measures and intended impact
    Action steps/tactics
    Clear timeline
    Resources outlined
    Plan for monitoring and communicating back to stakeholders

9. Consider using tools to help you operationalize your plan: dashboards, communication, adaptability, providing the right resources, and monitoring performance of those accountable for execution.

Action Steps

1. Identify how the organization could benefit from some intentional planning.
2. Notice how you feel about getting started, and discuss this with a team member who is likely to help champion the effort.
3. Together, outline what you need to get started and make a first draft of a timeline.
4. Determine who/what group is best positioned to lead the process. Is it a simple plan you can carry out yourself, or a more comprehensive effort that will benefit from a committee approach?
5. Schedule your next day off…now.

PART THREE

APPLYING THE IMPACT TRIANGLE TO STRONG BOARDS THAT CARE

3

CHAPTER TEN

FRIEND OR FOE?

THE RELATIONSHIP BETWEEN the executive director and the board, specifically the board president, presents an interesting dynamic. The executive director is hired as an expert in the nonprofit field, and the volunteer serving as president supervises and evaluates the executive director's performance. The president rotates in and out, and typically is not an expert in the field. Now, this dynamic absolutely can work, but why do I see both executive directors and board presidents getting a bit squeamish about this reporting relationship?

It comes back to the relationship thing. Regardless of what project you're working on, or what your role is, honoring the relationship you have with each other comes first. I often see board presidents back off because they feel bad for the poor, overworked executive director, and they think it's not the director's fault that performance is off track. Or the executive director shies away from asking "the boss" to follow up on that action she promised to deliver, because it's uncomfortable. Let's dig a little deeper.

Frame Expectations Early

These relationships don't have to be awkward. There's more work involved when there is a new executive director who has to get to know the whole board, and vice versa. But regardless of the situation, outline the way you like to work with each other up front. Over lunch one day, ask about how the other person likes to communicate, for example. I had a board president who liked to meet in person once a month; the next board president wanted a weekly email summary on key points. If I hadn't taken the time to ask, I probably would have been frustrating the board president without even knowing it.

And go further—talk about roles. Actually articulate that the board is expected to provide strategic direction, ensure the organization is well resourced (that's code for raising money), serve as ambassadors in the community, identify and recruit new members, and support staff in the implementation of plans. The executive director will hire and supervise the staff, manage operational issues (board members are not needed for handling the details), drive implementation of plans, and support the board in their work. And will the board president have the executive director's back when the executive needs advice or has to manage a politically sensitive issue?

These conversations are important even when the same people continue in the leadership positions. I recommend an annual check-in with straightforward dialogue.

Ask, and Ask Again, then Listen

I also recommend talking about the current board culture and how it's working.

- ▶ Is everyone's voice heard, or is there serious group think?
- ▶ Is the board engaged, or just going through the motions?
- ▶ Are roles and responsibilities clear?

Let it be known that you expect the work to be driven by the strategic plan and discuss how to monitor it. The board president should ask about what concerns the executive director has, or what challenges the organization is facing. It's important that board members and staff understand how others view the current situation and how well-positioned they are to move forward into a thriving future. This type of dialogue can lead to great strategic conversations and set the tone for how you will be successful partners.

Being self-aware and observant are key skills when building relationships. Not everyone is good at direct communication, so you may need to read between the lines. Do others seem reluctant to go deeper on a certain subject? Are they constantly redirecting the conversation? Some thoughtful open-ended questions may get to the bottom of the issue.

They Are People Too

Any strong relationship is built on trust and respect. The executive director and board will face some challenges together, as well as share in wonderful achievements. It is appropriate and sensible to get to know each other outside the boardroom. Make time for each other and learn about each other's families and interests. As you do, the relationships strengthen and carry over into your working relationship. Perhaps you like to boast about your kids, or dog, or athletic prowess. Whatever your personal interests, it feels good when someone asks about those things, right? When you genuinely care about someone, it's natural to check in on what's going on in that person's life.

Of course, you don't have to be best friends and pal around every weekend to earn the respect of a colleague. Actually, many people feel it's not professional to do so. They will give you signals about how much information they are comfortable sharing, so be observant.

Results

As the relationships grow, opportunities flourish. The executive director evaluation is no longer a period of tension or a surprise, but rather a chance for the board to look forward and support a dedicated employee. And the executive director isn't anxious about holding board members accountable, because the expectations have been set, trust has developed, and now it's just business.

Overlooking the value board members bring to the table is sometimes a shortcoming of staff. But making a sincere effort to understand their interests and talents can lead to a wonderful partnership. It will also result in highly engaged and productive board members who are bringing the mission alive. So set the bar high and help each other rise to the occasion.

"They" Aren't the Problem

I will let you in on a little secret. I cannot tolerate it when I hear leaders talk about how board members won't do something. I hear it from both staff and other board members. There—it's out...I suppose I need to work on that, but for now let's focus on what to do about the perceived issue regarding volunteers.

Keep in mind that when we focus on our mindset and the relationship, positive results come much faster. There are a few things we need to believe first in order to make progress toward the goal of volunteers performing in the manner we desire. Let's use the example of fundraising, since it seems to be a popular concern.

First, yes, board members will fundraise. Your volunteers have joined the board or the committee because they want to help the community by working with your organization. They have chosen you; they trust you to do good work and want to work alongside you. How great is that? All this free talent and passion ready to help you! They want to help and be the catalyst for good. Remember that.

There are many ways for board members to get involved in fundraising. Not everyone will be equipped to ask for the $25,000 gift. But everyone can ask for smaller gifts, or introduce you to someone who is very influential, or host a non-ask event. So, we don't get to presume the volunteers are stubborn, or lazy, or too busy. Did you hear that? They aren't too busy! It is very common to fall back on that excuse. Our volunteers probably *are* busy, but remember that they chose to work with you and they will make time for the organization, to the extent they can, when they are well equipped with information and tools.

If you have found yourself falling into this trap of making assumptions about why board members aren't rising to the occasion, stop and think about it for a minute. Focus. Picture them at a campaign meeting, asking for a donation or telling the story of the impact your organization makes. What if you believed they can and will fundraise? What if you supported them instead of criticizing them? What is possible then? Anything.

Secondly, let's look at your relationship with these volunteers. Very often we think that when people don't rise to the occasion, it's because they lack motivation. In some cases that may be true. But what if it's something else? What have you done to find out the reason for lack of participation? When you have a strong relationship with people, it's fairly easy to ask them how they are feeling about their participation and how you may support them in their efforts.

I have done this many times, and invariably I hear things like "I don't know how," or "I'm not feeling very confident," or "I don't understand why we need to do this." It's as if a light bulb goes on over my head! Somewhere along the line we've missed some important communication. However we delivered the message, it wasn't received. Notice that they didn't say they didn't want to fundraise. They indicated that they didn't know how, or the psychology of it was getting to them (fear and lack of confidence), or it didn't seem like a priority.

Here's the good news when you hear responses like that: all that can be fixed. You can teach board members how to fundraise and give them the necessary tools, which will boost their confidence. And you can spend the time to carefully explain why the donated funds are so critical to the mission. *The piece that needs to be in place is the relationship.* By supporting volunteers with tools and effective communication, you are engaging them and building a stronger relationship. Ideally, you will have started on the path early in your interaction, and they already trust you.

Once your board members feel motivated and confident, they will be serving in a grander way. They will feel valued because they understand they have a significant role to play that directly impacts the community. So really examine your mindset to see if you are thinking and behaving like someone with a positive attitude toward your board members' potential. Then look at your relationship with the board members individually. Volunteers are a gift and when you utilize the Impact Triangle, you will build a strong foundation for success.

CHAPTER ELEVEN

WE ARE THE CHAMPIONS

I LOVE THAT SONG by Queen! It speaks of perseverance and fighting to the end. This social enterprise stuff can be tough, but we can help ourselves by lining up a strong team of advocates. Here is how it applies to developing a strong board.

We are going to focus on recruiting the right board members, engaging them, and creating effective committee work. Now, regardless of what segment of that work you are currently focused on, you need allies. None of us can be successful alone, at least not for long.

So you need to line up your team using these four steps:

1. Identify two or three board members who you believe understand the importance of this project, who are respected by other board members, and who you see as being ready to help assist in the change.
2. Explain your reasoning and let them know you need their help in setting this new direction.
3. Ask for a commitment from them. They will probably ask some great questions, so be sure you have your ducks in a row, as it's hard to sell a half-baked idea.

4. Coach them, if needed, on how to effectively communicate the change to the rest of the board.

Whenever you undertake a shift from how things have been done, there will most likely be some level of resistance, as we've already discussed in chapter 6. It doesn't necessarily mean people are opposed to the change; it may simply be that they are having trouble letting go of the old way. A few champions who have bought into the new way, and who are respected by others, can decrease the odds of ongoing, high-level resistance. Sincere and active listening plays a key role here, too. All the while, keep the plans moving forward, though some empathy and patience may be required.

When it's time to discuss the newly redesigned orientation plan, for example, have a peer volunteer start the conversation and set the tone. It can be powerful for others to hear from someone they respect and trust who has been in their shoes. The team of champions you expect to be involved in implementation must be ready to discuss what is possible by doing the orientation in a different way.

I strongly recommend this strategy of identifying champions when you are striving to influence a new direction. But don't stop there. You will need champions most of the time to help you lead your work. It is applicable to all types of board work, as well as staff situations. Be curious and bold. Who knows what great things can happen when you try something new?

CHAPTER TWELVE

SIX STEPS TO RECRUIT THE BEST

BEFORE WE GET STARTED, let's get on the same page regarding who is responsible for board recruitment. The answer is the whole board, and the board governance committee (sometimes known as the nominating committee, or the board development committee) provides oversight. The executive director plays a critical role, and I am assuming the executive director is on the committee. Also, the current or incoming president of the board is a key member of this group. The committee is tasked with monitoring the year-round process. (Yes, it is a year-round process.) Every board member is expected to participate. And the president needs to keep this topic in front of the board. So with the combination of the governance committee's work, the president's prioritization, the executive director's management, and a sustainable process, board development can be very successful.

As mentioned earlier, if a structured process has not been in place, it would be preferable to have identified a champion or two to help influence the shift. There will be grumbles from some people about not knowing anyone to nominate, and that's understandable. Assuring them that you can equip them with tools to be involved in supporting the critical goal of board development may help boost their confidence. So think positive. Bringing energized, talented people into the fold should be exciting!

1. Assess Current Board and Outline Needs

By now you have completed a strategic planning process. So you know where the organization is going and who you need on the team, right? If your big-picture initiatives have not been well framed, then stop. It is very difficult to recruit the right volunteers if you aren't clear on what you are trying to accomplish. Go back and read chapters 7 through 9.

Moving on…now that everyone is clear on the strategic goals of your business, let's get serious about defining winning criteria needed to ensure success. An intentional recruiting strategy will serve you well. Most of us have experienced the shotgun approach, where we just grab any people who show interest, tell them the mission, and hope for the best. And then we wonder why board retention is poor. It's time to change things up—approach recruitment differently and you can expect different results.

I think it's empowering to have the entire board go through an exercise of listing the criteria for an ideal board member. This can be done in twenty to thirty minutes at a regularly scheduled meeting. Utilize an experienced facilitator who will refer to the goals that need to be accomplished over the next two to three years (a typical board term). Then ask what characteristics and traits board members would need to ensure achievement of these goals. Who can contribute the talent, resources, and passion the organization needs to implement the plan?

For example, if there is a capital expansion on the horizon, then perhaps an architect, general contractor, someone connected to affluent people, a well-respected leader who could lead a campaign, would all make the list of desired attributes. If outreach is a goal, who lives beyond the current service area? If there is a need to improve the image of the business, then maybe a person who has ties to a public relations expert would be beneficial. It's always good to consider folks who have a different sphere of influence than the current members, too. And while it's assumed you'll be recruiting folks who are passionate about the mission and share the organization's values, it can't hurt to list those criteria.

I can't emphasize enough how valuable it is to have a diverse set of volunteers leading the organization. Look at age, gender, geography (do they all live in the same community?), industry, life experience, balance of visionaries and tacticians, and cultural backgrounds. A diverse board is a strong board that appreciates different perspectives and moves forward together faster. Be sure to include criteria that will enhance diversity on the list.

Once your board members have exhausted their ideas, it's time to prioritize the list by identifying where there are gaps. First, you need to assess the current composition of the board. *Here is the catch:* as you are instructing the board members on the process, ask them to keep in mind that you are not just evaluating whether members possess certain talents or connections. You are evaluating whether they are *using* that talent, or introducing their friends and others to the organization. If they aren't participating in fundraising, their capacity to do so doesn't matter.

Being sensitive to the dynamic in the room is essential. You don't want to offend anyone who thinks the board is already perfect as it is. But all boards have areas in which they can grow. Coach the facilitator to choose his or her words carefully.

Then tell board members that they each get a certain number of votes (three to five works well, depending on the size of the group). Ask them to place their votes with a check mark next to the characteristics on the list that they feel are most needed based on current gaps in desired composition. They can place all their votes on the same characteristic or split them any way they wish. Once that multi-vote exercise is complete, several characteristics will likely stand out. Circle the top six to eight with the most votes, and bingo! Now you have a list of the desired criteria in board candidates who can lead the organization toward the stated goals. This can all typically be done in less than an hour.

Note: You may be familiar with a matrix that has the desired board member criteria across the top, and then the name of each current board member down the left side (see next page). With a predetermined goal in mind relevant to the number of members you desire in each category, you move across the chart and check any box that describes the volunteer. You will be able to see which characteristics are well represented on the current board, and which ones are not. This matrix is very specific and should be created in a separate meeting by the executive director and board president, as it contains sensitive information that should be discussed confidentially.

Name	Previous Board Experience	Marketing Expertise	Connected to Affluence	Fundraising Experience	Lives in Untapped Market	Leadership Experience
Sue	X		X	X		
Dan	X		X	X		
Pam		X	X			X
Lezli	X			X		X
Ken			X	X		X
Steve	X			X		X
Corey			X	X	X	X

2. Identify—No Stone Left Unturned

I wish I had a dollar for every time I heard executive directors or board presidents say they can't go back to their board members to provide ideas for board prospects because they don't have any more names to give. Well, if you believe that, then it will be a self-fulfilling prophecy. So we're going to look at it differently. This can be the beginning of a stronger, more successful recruitment plan.

What if you helped them look at it differently and they could utilize new sources? And what about the new board members who came on last year who haven't been asked to participate in the recruitment process yet? Let's give them some tools to use so they can feel engaged in the process, becoming productive and thereby valued.

First, it might be a fun group activity to just brainstorm what groups of people they know, such as neighbors, family, members of book clubs or poker groups, colleagues, fellow churchgoers, service club members, parents of their kids' friends, members of online social or professional networks, members of other volunteer groups, fellow alumni, donors, folks from the dog park, vendors, etc. The list of informal or formal categories and groups of people can be almost endless. Doing this, without a lot of parameters, builds energy around the idea that they *do* actually know many people in a variety of ways. And let's remember to reach out to past board members, who understand board expectations quite well, and see who they might add to the list of nominees.

Tip: As you go through your days, try to remember that with almost every person you interact with, you should ask that person whom he or she would recommend you consider as a nominee. Inform these people of the organization's future plans and key initiatives, and summarize the type of people you desire. Your network will expand vastly, and soon you'll be connected to more people than you imagined.

Not everyone will be able to point you to a great prospect, but now all those people you talked to know the goals of the organization and understand that you take board recruitment seriously. Without exception, you will also add these folks to your newsletter list so the organization will be top of mind. And who knows... if they aren't already, perhaps they will become donors and/or advocates for you. Remember, people are generous and want to help.

Let's explore the internet option a bit. By the time this book goes to print, who knows what programs will be trending? But for now, I'll reference Facebook, Twitter, LinkedIn, and Pinterest. Most of your current board members will be active on at least one of these sites. If they were willing to simply look at their friends, followers, and connections and give thought to who might make a good nominee, that could be quite beneficial. And if they took it a step farther, and used the search feature on LinkedIn, they could select by company or group. With the advanced feature, they can identify people they have connections with who they might not have even realized were well matched for consideration.

Additionally, LinkedIn now has a Board Connect function that will identify volunteers looking to serve with organizations that match their interests. Here is a great example of how it worked for Caroline Nassif from her LinkedIn post on March 27, 2013:

Last year was a HUGE year for me. I got married, finished a big project at work, and became a licensed California Architect after 5 years of grueling exams. As the New Year approached, I mourned the loss of my big goals. I realized that I suddenly had a lot more time, and wanted to do something meaningful with it.

I'm sure this is when you expect me to say "LinkedIn to the rescue!" Well, that's exactly what happened, but not quite the way you might imagine.

As a young professional, I had dutifully filled out my LinkedIn profile, thinking that it would come in handy as I sought to expand my professional network. I actually had no idea that LinkedIn could be a resource for nonprofit board opportunities. So when I received an InMail from Terrie Light, the Executive Director of the Berkeley Food and Housing Project, about their search for a new Board Member, I was pleasantly surprised. Little did she know I was actually looking for her (inadvertently)! I responded to Terrie and scheduled a time to meet.

As the day of our meeting drew closer, I began to get nervous. Was I cut out to be on the Board of Directors for such an amazing nonprofit? Why would they want an architect on their board anyway? The position sounded like it required many years of experience, something I didn't have. I started to wonder if Terrie had the right person. I looked over my LinkedIn profile again to make sure that it was clear that I am a young professional. Could it be that Terrie really found *my* profile interesting?

When I met with Terrie, she explained that she was looking for a younger board member with lots of energy—someone who could engage with the more experienced professionals on the board and add to their efforts. She also explained that one of their goals is to build a new building: a multi-use homeless shelter, transitional housing, clinic, and counseling center to serve their clients. An architect with my experience could help them as they issued an RFP, refined their building program, and interviewed architects. This was very exciting for me because I immediately saw it as a learning opportunity as well as something I was primed to do from past experience. I had worked for 7 years at an affordable housing architecture firm, and had also volunteered in public advocacy campaigns for similar types of projects in the past.

A few months later, after meeting with other board members and attending a board meeting, I was voted unanimously on the board: a match I could not have better engineered if I tried. As I begin my service on the board, I'm excited, honored, and grateful for my new meaningful connection.

3. Nominate

Now that we know the kind of people we need, and where we can find them, it's time to nominate them. I suggest using a form to capture all the information we know about a nominee. Some useful data points are:

- Company and position
- Where they reside
- Which of the outlined ideal criteria they represent
- Previous volunteer experience
- Any connection with the organization
- What committee might be a good match
- Have they expressed any interest in becoming involved?
- To what *different* individuals or groups are they connected?
- How well do they fit with the culture?

You get the picture. Try to zero in on the key elements that will allow the governance committee to make good decisions.

Note: Do not tell nominees they are being considered! On average, only one-third of nominees actually end up joining boards. Sometimes it's because they never get on the A list, sometimes there is an abundance of amazing nominees and not enough seats open, and other times they just aren't interested. Once a person knows he or she has been nominated, it creates a certain tension. Let's try to avoid the creation of an awkward situation if we can, in case the nominee is never approached for candidacy.

Once a sufficient amount of initial information is obtained on a nominee, it gets submitted to the executive director or governance committee for consideration. From there, the nominees are vetted against the key criteria to determine who may be the best match for the board.

4. Vet the Nominees

There are several ways to vet the nominees that all get the same result—a prioritized list of highly desirable board candidates. This crucial step is often overlooked. It's troubling, but I see it happen because the process is rushed, or everyone knows Joe is a really nice guy so he automatically gets a nod, or there is simply a lack of experience in the group. Keep in mind that there really is an obligation on the part of the committee to invest time in a thoughtful process that will result in a stronger board. The organization's strategic goals must be supported enthusiastically by stakeholders who understand the seriousness of achieving them. To haphazardly start contacting candidates would be a mistake.

It is the role of the governance committee to process all nominations. One way to approach the ranking or vetting process is to devote the majority of a committee meeting to this process after the nomination deadline has passed, then have the list of ideal criteria in plain view, as well as a summary sheet of all nominees. This summary would include key points for all nominees, including profession, residence, volunteer experience, what characteristics they align with, and who knows them and how well, etc.

Sometimes a committee will weight the desired criteria. For example, if a nominee lives in an underrepresented community, that could be worth one point; if he or she is connected to many affluent people, that may be worth two points. Once the ranking system is established, each nominee is assigned a number based on points earned. Additional discussion takes place, because there may be information available outside the data on the form. For example, perhaps someone is rotating off another board and so the timing may seem right to approach him, assuming he lines up well against desired criteria.

Keep in mind that typically three candidates are needed for every available seat, so the committee will select an A list with at least that number of required candidates. The B list typically consists of wonderful nominees about whom you may need more information, or who align with fewer of the desired characteristics than those on the A list. I use these terms cautiously, and you can come up with your own terms. It should never be implied that any one nominee is better or worse than another. At certain times, in different situations, most nominees would make an A list. The process is just like hiring an employee—you are looking for the best-matched candidates for the job.

A note here about perspective and relationships. We're walking through the technical process now, but how you approach the process and how well you know the candidates are also crucial. (*Psssst*—by the way, having volunteers go through this process together has another benefit: they become more engaged and have a deeper sense of ownership in the process. Additionally, they are getting to know each other better and strengthening their relationships!) This process is pretty dynamic, but it's possible to feel bogged down, especially if recruitment hasn't been approached like this before. Trust the process. It will yield good results. However, you must stay focused and persevere to remain on course. Just picture those future board meetings and events with many committed and engaged volunteers accomplishing amazing things. Your work will be rewarded.

Let's move on to the next step, where we'll address the relationship side of things.

5. Interview

It's generally not a good idea to ask someone to marry you without some type of courtship period. Same here—you won't be asking candidates to join the board without some cultivation of the relationship. Remember that one of the cornerstones of this book about the Impact Triangle is the power of relationships. That's why it is a good idea to understand who knows the candidate and how well. It's not uncommon for us to go outside the board and ask others we know to make an introduction.

If candidates have no previous exposure to the organization, then invite them for a tour, to an event, or perhaps to breakfast with the executive director. Start engaging them when the only agenda is to get them acquainted with the organization and people involved. It typically doesn't take long to get an impression of their level of interest in the organization. They may not even take a meeting. And if they just aren't that into you, accept it and move on—you have more candidates on the list. And it's not personal. Put yourself in their shoes. There is no way you could serve well on the boards of all the worthy organizations in town. At some point, we all have to choose.

If all signs are pointing toward a fairly high level of interest with a candidate, then it's time for the recruitment interview. The reason it's called an interview is because both parties are gaining insight and information during this meeting. I feel strongly that the executive director should attend every one of these meetings. There should be a common denominator for comparative purposes, and to ensure the key components of the interview are included each time. Additionally, a board member should be present to provide the volunteer perspective. Many times, this will be the person who made the nomination and has the strongest relationship with the candidate. It is also a good idea to keep the full board abreast of who is being interviewed, as the board will be voting on these folks in the future.

These interviews can take place at your office, over coffee, or in any setting you consider appropriate. The venue is less important than the content. You will want to bring along some collateral materials if you haven't already provided them, including an annual report, an overview of programs, a board roster, and most importantly, the written expectations of a board member. The conversation will likely develop organically, but below is an example of things to keep in mind:

- ▶ Establish rapport.
- ▶ Thank candidates for their interest in getting more involved in the organization.
- ▶ The executive director provides an overview of the organizational structure, mission and values, and strategic goals.
- ▶ Board members tell their story of how and why they got involved and what has been rewarding to them.
- ▶ Ask candidates some probing questions about their background and experience to gain additional information and confirm what is known.
- ▶ Always ask why they are interested in considering joining the board.
- ▶ Review the written expectations of a board member—be specific about time expectations, financial contributions, advocacy, legal responsibilities, etc. Candidates should be asking you questions along the way—it's a red flag if they don't, because you want to ensure they have understood and retained key points. They will want to "interview" you as well.
- ▶ Ask them questions like, "How comfortable would you feel inviting someone you know to lunch with the executive director to learn more about the organization?" Possessing desired traits isn't enough—they must be willing to participate.
- ▶ Provide an overview of the various committees.

- If feeling confident about the match, tell the nominee why you think he or she would be a strong candidate—be specific. This is key! If candidates don't understand why you think they align well with the values and goals of the organization, it will take longer to engage them.
- Ask candidates what they hope to get out of the experience.
- Review the selection process with them along with the timeline, and explain how orientation will be conducted, if they join the board.

At some point, and it could be at this interview meeting if you know the candidate well, you will ask for permission to advance the person's name to the governance committee for approval. Quite often the candidate will want to discuss the possibility with a spouse, or just take a few days to digest the information. Frankly, I respect that, because I want to be sure candidates are really committed and feeling confident about their decision before bringing them onto the board. This relates to perspective.

By having a formal process in place for board recruitment, not only do you set a tone of professionalism, but you are adopting a true selection process that you believe matches the best people to serve the organization at the time. Don't settle for less. This businesslike approach will set you apart and people will be honored to serve.

6. Select and Approve

As the interviews are being conducted, feed reactions back to the governance committee. Once all interviews are complete, the committee will create a new class of members for board approval. A note on timing here: ideally, identification and cultivation of potential board members are taking place year-round. Then the actual act of interviewing and selecting can occur over the course of sixty to ninety days. After this, the formal orientation takes place, and all members of the rookie class come on board simultaneously.

In reality, sometimes we find ourselves in a position of recruiting and selecting throughout the year. This isn't the best scenario for the new members who have now missed a portion of the board year, and who may not feel as though they are really a part of the group. It can be done, but the most effective way for both the organization and the new member is to start the new class all together. Getting off on the right track is important, because you might not get another chance to win people back. Remember—relationships matter, and one of the top reasons volunteers stay involved is because of the social aspect of the organization.

How the governance committee determines who will be in the new class is clear at this point. The top candidates have been approached, and they have indicated whether they would like to join the board or not. Another possibility is that the interview didn't go well, and now you're second-guessing the choice. If cultivation was done well, this isn't likely to happen. However, if you find yourself in this conundrum, it's important to be honest. Would a committee position be a better fit? If you aren't comfortable with the candidate now, chances are the situation will only get worse. It's better to leave a seat vacant if there isn't another suitable candidate than to select a person who isn't well positioned to advance the mission.

Each organization has bylaws that outline the process for approving board members. Typically a slate is presented to the full board for a vote, and many times this occurs at the annual meeting. Since the new members may be in attendance, it is suggested that you email a summary of candidates' biographies to the board in advance for review and invite questions prior to the annual meeting.

And there you are—with a brand-new class of eager volunteers ready to raise money, advocate, work in committees, plan strategic initiatives, and direct policy decisions. This can be a very exciting time! As we know, your perspective and the strength of your relationships will determine how successful you will be during execution. I believe you will be a whopping success.

Calendar

I often get asked about the timing of these steps. I would recommend you work backwards from your annual meeting or the first board meeting of the year. So an annual timeline could look something like this:

- ► Assess current board composition and outline needs – October
- ► Start identifying potential board members – October through April
- ► Committee accepts nominees – October through April

- Committee vets nominees – February through April
- Top candidates are interviewed – April and May
- New class of board members is recommended to the board – June (annual meeting)
- New board member orientation – August
- First board meeting of the year – September

Every organization is different and will create its own timeline. The important thing is to have a deliberate, sustainable process to ensure a strong board, using the Impact Triangle as a guide.

CHAPTER THIRTEEN

WHERE ARE THE YOUNG ONES?

IF YOU LOOK AROUND the boardroom and everyone is of a similar age, it's past time to address age diversity. Rather than worry about the correct label, such as Gen Y or Millennial, let's just focus on the people who best match the organization's needs. We have already talked about the value of a diversified board, but a question I get asked often is, "How do we recruit younger board members?" The answer is very similar to how you recruit anyone, but you may need to look in different places.

With any new member, cultivating the relationship is a critical step in the recruitment process. We've been over that...and I have noticed that when an older person thinks about approaching a significantly younger person, there is a different kind of tension in the air. What is that? If you have felt it yourself, stop and think about it for a minute and try to understand what triggered that feeling. It could be that you weren't sure if you would be able to relate well to someone younger. But young people are just regular people too, so adjust your mindset and move forward.

You may decide you aren't the best person to get to know this individual, and that is a normal part of any recruitment strategy. You always want to have the most "right" person start the conversation. I would encourage you not to avoid the situation altogether; who knows what you could learn? And this could be a future peer volunteer, so you will want to build a relationship at some point anyway. Stop and examine your feelings on the subject, and imagine the possibilities.

Where do you find these enthusiastic people who are committed to the social sector and were born more recently than you? Before you read the list below, keep in mind that age cannot be the only factor in nominating a candidate—that person must bring something else to the table on the desired trait list. You are committed to enrolling the best-matched candidates, so avoid recruiting younger members just for the sake of recruiting younger members.

Here are some places to consider when you are identifying younger board members:

▸ Look at your internal circle, including donors, volunteers, participants, vendors, friends of employees, friends of current board members' children, etc.

▸ LinkedIn Board Connect. As mentioned previously, in 2012 LinkedIn launched a program that has been helpful to nonprofits and is free when you enter your organization's tax identification number. It allows you to leverage your connections to find talented people who may meet your criteria and be interested in volunteering.

▸ YNPN, the Young Nonprofit Professional Network, is an association of people that is committed to building networking and professional development, as well as connecting members to the community. They are looking to volunteer! Most major cities have chapters, so google away and learn how to connect.

▸ College leadership programs are also sources for motivated younger men and women who are eager to make their mark. Many times they have had to complete a service project, and are therefore familiar with the nonprofit sector. Additionally, more universities now offer degrees or certificates in Nonprofit Management. By contacting your local university or community college, you can learn how best to get connected with future leaders.

▸ Look to see if your local Chamber of Commerce has a young professional group. If so, see how you can get an audience—by speaking, attending a mixer, etc.

▸ Americorps is another source for younger, socially committed leaders. This federal program engages them in community service work with nonprofits. As a result, these folks are likely in tune with the reality of what it takes to succeed and have benefitted from strong learning experiences.

When you are strategizing about how you can further diversify your board, keep in mind that you will need to be flexible. It's easy to stereotype younger people as those who want immediate gratification, are techno-savvy, and move on if they don't see quick benefits. Okay, well, let's say those things are true for some younger men and women. Is that a bad thing? Is your thinking stuck? Let's look at it another way.

I would love to have people involved in my organization who are social media experts! Many organizations have at least put their big toe into the water when it comes to having an online presence. But I'll speak for the slightly older population—we didn't grow up with technology, so we are less familiar, and therefore unless we have made a real effort, it stands to say we have not all taken a giant leap into the deep end when it comes to social media. And if most of the executive directors are older, that could be a problem. Suppose you welcomed a new board member who is experienced in the use of technology for marketing purposes, and that person joined the marketing committee or worked alongside staff to develop a marketing plan. Your new member could engage quickly and have a greater chance of being satisfied by his or her contribution right away.

It does seem that this younger generation wants to learn and develop skills while serving. From my perspective, that's such a big win! It means they will be less hesitant to move outside their comfort zone and will strive to help in areas of need, even if they lack experience. Consider all the skills your organization needs to be successful—program development, fiscal oversight, legal expertise, marketing, community development, raising funds, etc. As with any board member, talk about the needs of the community when recruiting young people, and see where there might be a match—and where they might be willing to participate and learn. And here's a thought: if you have a project moving particularly slowly and can't seem to get any traction, put a young person in charge of it. If it's true the young want results quickly, this could be a wonderful opportunity.

I read somewhere that the millennial generation is very committed to giving back, much like "the Greatest Generation" back in the day. Other experts have argued they are more self-focused and narcissistic. I choose to believe each person is an individual, and like people of any age, young people will volunteer and serve in a way that works best for them.

So you need to be able to roll with it. Welcome new ideas, talk to other board members about the culture you have created, and ask if it needs to change. When you provide an environment where all people and ideas are welcome, and where a person can truly contribute to the overall cause, you are well positioned to attract and retain great volunteers from all walks of life.

CHAPTER FOURTEEN

BOARD MEMBER EXPECTATIONS

THE CORPORATION CODE IN your state will outline what the legal governance responsibilities are for a nonprofit board of directors. I'll include a few notes about that at the end of this section, but since there seem to be more issues in regard to the ability to effectively communicate expectations to the individual board member, I will focus there. You need to be able to see three levels—the organization/board as a whole; then the working team/committees; and finally the individual board member—in order to ensure you are communicating well at all levels.

When I get a call to work with a board and help them deal with an issue, the vast majority of the time there is some connection to unclear expectations. Either there is a lack of understanding or muddled communication. So let's tackle this and look at how to convey expectations.

The board is responsible for setting the organization's *strategic direction, for ensuring the mission and purpose is served, and for the financial health* of the organization. It is not easy to boil that down into simple language for a new member, but it is critical to do just that so there are no surprises. Unfortunately, we tend to be a little nervous about being specific when it comes to fundraising expectations. Why is that? We are afraid of something, it seems. Afraid the new volunteers won't accept their nomination if they have to ask for money? Afraid they will refuse to raise funds even if they accept the nomination? Afraid we will offend them somehow? I encourage you to take a look at your mindset, with the Impact Triangle in mind.

Think about why these volunteers joined the board. They want to make a positive impact on the community, right? There will be other rewarding moments for them, including expanding their network, but initially they are mostly eager to affect social issues. In order to do so, they want direction and guidance. They really do want to be told honestly about the direct work to be done, as well as the softer expectations. They want to rise to the occasion, so raise the bar. As you reflect, try to ensure you are not blocking their success. You owe it to them to give it to them straight.

When you do, their doubts can be expressed, and you will have an opportunity to discuss how you will support them. Also, many board candidates are already donors to some organization. Maybe they have even invited others to participate at some point. They could actually be in a position to leverage their experience to help other board members. So don't sell them short—it isn't fair. It is essential you see that new members receive complete information, regardless of what it is, concerning expectations. Otherwise, how can you expect anything from them?

So if board members are expected to work strategically at a high level, how do you turn the somewhat abstract (provide direction, serve mission, etc.) into tangible and measurable actions?

First, think about what success looks like. Who are the board members you feel are really participating at a high level and achieving key goals? What are they doing to meet expectations? They probably show up at meetings, follow up on committee tasks, get involved in some way with fundraising, and perhaps share new ideas. What else?

Every organization will have its own set of expectations. Below is a list of things you may want to consider including in your written document, with a couple of things to add at the top:

Reports to: board president (*many board members think they report to the executive director*)
Term: three years renewable, starting July 2014 (*for example*)

- Passionately commit to the mission and goals of the organization.
- Attend meetings of the board of directors on the third Tuesday of the month at 7:00 a.m., September through June.
- Serve on a committee and actively participate in meetings.
- Contribute expertise, participate, and monitor the strategic planning and goals of the organization.
- Contribute generously with an annual financial investment to the organization at the Founders Club level. (Notice you will be specific to at least the range of gift expected—see Board solicitation section in chapter 24 to learn more.)
- Follow conflict of interest rules, confidentiality policies, and all other governance practices and procedures.
- Assist the board in carrying out its fiduciary responsibilities, by reviewing the organization's annual financial statements and recommending resource development strategies.
- Assist in building a strong board by identifying and nominating board candidates who match the current needs of the organization, and support the strategic initiatives.
- Develop funding support by identifying donor prospects, making introductions, articulating the case for support, securing gifts, and stewarding donors.
- Attend scheduled board retreats, planning meetings, workshops, or other board development activities.
- Attend and support the annual special event by selling tickets, securing auction items and/or sponsors.
- Represent the organization and serve as an advocate.
- Support a culture that encourages board members to ask questions, and challenge assumptions that may not directly serve the mission.

Once you have invited a volunteer to serve on the board, have the person sign this statement of expectations and date it. Periodically, you may revise expectations, and at that time you will want all members to sign a new version. It is a good way to remind the veterans of their role, too.

From the legal standpoint, assuming your organization sought counsel and created articles of incorporation and meaningful bylaws, I suggest you review these documents every two to three years. Typically, the bylaws will outline:

- Required officer positions, their duties, and how they may be elected
- The authority the board has been given
- Number of board members allowed, term limits, and how they may be approved
- Required committees, allowable committees, and methods for forming them
- Meeting parameters (when, where, quorum, annual meetings, etc.)
- Indemnification factors, and directors' and officers' insurance
- Other fun stuff like annual report, contracts, and fiscal year determination

I am no longer surprised to hear "I don't know" when I ask leadership how many board members are allowed to serve. Bylaws are boring, but responsible governance requires them to be reviewed every few years. The board has fiduciary responsibility for the organization and therefore needs to understand these details. Try conducting a trivia contest at a board meeting to educate members on key points. They will do nearly anything for prizes.

Look also for policies in your board handbook about *duty of care* (they commit to being active and informed), *loyalty* (they commit to put the interest of the organization above their own), and *honesty* (they commit to compliance). Everything from a Conflict of Interest policy to record retention requirements is included within these policies. If you can't locate your board handbook, or are unsure about how to develop one, contact your local management services organization (MSO) or nonprofit technical support organization for guidance.

I encourage you to review your written expectations, or create them if you need to, so you can start out by building trust with your new board members. This is a function of the board development (or governance) committee, by the way. And keeping the Impact Triangle in mind, now that you are ready to approach the setting of expectations from a positive perspective, you will engage board members in meaningful conversation right from the start.

CHAPTER FIFTEEN

WANNA GET ENGAGED?

WE HAVE ALREADY OUTLINED the reasons why relationships matter. When it comes to board members, the relationship is crucial. Your board members are volunteers. They are happy to serve the community through your organization. And they deserve to be appreciated and respected. To that end, bringing them into the fold should be a deliberate process by which you move them from a rookie and perhaps tentative contributor, to a more engaged participant who is fully active, to a leader on the board who can mentor others.

It intrigues me how common it is to see an executive director incredibly frustrated by the lack of involvement from board members. They complain about board members' minimal involvement in fundraising, low attendance at meetings, or lack of communication and response when contacted, etc. This really shouldn't be a surprise given the typically small amount of attention paid by staff and other board members to honest engagement strategies. Now, if we embrace what's been said already about relationships, the gap will be easier to bridge. It is the executive director's responsibility to have a plan to engage board members. A plan isn't difficult to implement when done right. And when volunteers are engaged, the work doesn't all fall on the executive director's shoulders. It's pretty cool how it works that way. So let's figure out how to get started.

First, let me clarify one thing: while it is the executive director's job to ensure there is an engagement and retention plan, the governance committee discusses the recommendations and actively supports the process. Engagement isn't a big secret, and it's good to have members understand that their degree of involvement and satisfaction matters to you. When you convey that sincere commitment to them, you will have already taken a step toward retention. (Notice that I will use the words *engagement* and *retention* interchangeably—one results in the other.)

You will have already started engaging board members through the cultivation and recruitment process. You have told them why they were selected, and how you need their experience, connections, and time to help advance the organization's mission. They are feeling enthusiastic, needed, and revved up to go! There are many activities that will strategically increase engagement, so let's review some here.

Meaningful Orientation

A new member's learning curve is not conquered with a one-time session, but a formal orientation should still occur. It is most appropriate to have the board president lead it, with support from the executive director and president elect, or another tenured board member. As I have already mentioned, it is most effective to have all new members attend the session together as one class.

Now, I'm no Einstein, but even I know that if a meeting has lackluster materials, or the information is presented in a monotone, or there seems to be no clear agenda or direction—guess what? The audience won't be paying attention for long and will start returning emails on their phones. Mission not accomplished. And I know this because in my first executive director job, I agreed to help facilitate the new board member orientation using the same design and materials from the previous year. And then…I thought I was going to poke out my eyeballs. Now, I had updated a few things and enhanced the appearance of the handouts, but I had no idea how flat the event would fall.

My very wonderful board president just read from the notes or PowerPoint. The material related to financial reports, bylaws, history of the organization, organizational structure, etc. I looked around the room, and the five new members were either politely staring at him with glazed eyes and an occasional nod or were thumbing ahead, hoping that something more scintillating was hidden in the pages. I was mortified for wasting their precious time and looked for ideas to spice up the session.

At the very end, I went off script and started asking the new members questions about what they wanted to get out of their board experience, how they best liked to communicate, etc. It certainly didn't offset the damage already done, but I was hoping the orientation would at least end on a higher note. However, I knew the goal of the orientation did not get met. The lesson was to never assume a plan that you had no part in preparing is good enough; always review, practice, and invest time in ensuring a top-notch experience. The orientation will be only as good as the preparation put into the planning.

So, what is the best format to ensure an orientation is inspiring and instructive? There are several goals to consider:

- Start building relationships among board members, because they need to bond in order to work together as a team.
- Be perceived as professional and make a good impression.
- Discuss key information on the organization and its culture so new members have a strong foundation on which to make good decisions and understand how business is conducted.
- Provide the necessary overview of legal documents and responsibilities so they clearly understand their fiduciary responsibilities.
- Carefully review board member expectations and roles.

In terms of how to disseminate the information, I prefer to post most information online and/or email it in advance so we don't need to spend time on the less critical items. The members can review this information in advance, and then spend the majority of the orientation discussing the most critical content. Allowing time for participants' questions is important. Many organizations provide a binder with all the printed documents as well. I find this to be a waste of paper, frankly, but I do agree that hard copies of key documents may be a good idea. What those are is up to you.

I can't stress enough that using your board members' time wisely is serious. It's important for the board president to attend and have at least a small part on the agenda. But if that person isn't an effective and dynamic facilitator, give him or her a small part at the top of the agenda, then utilize others who are better suited for a great presentation. Remember those boring lectures in school? Same idea. And if you know anything about adult learning theory, we learn primarily by doing (kinesthetically). Some of us are also auditory learners (we like lectures and groups discussions), while others are visual learners (we like maps, charts, videos, and colors). To increase the odds that the new board members will retain any of the information, use a combination of strategies and focus on how you can make the session experiential.

You must include active group discussion. Ask the new members for ideas on certain topics, have them practice explaining the mission to a partner or use some other participatory technique. And even if you are anti-PowerPoint, utilize some type of visuals, such as videos or maps, to assist learning. In addition, when board members are told *why* things are done a certain way, they tend to better understand and behave consistently. Get your new board members participating in a way that will enhance learning! And by the way, nobody likes to sit very long, so a little moving around, which could be as simple as switching seats, is also a good idea.

In terms of content, there are some standard things to include:

▸ Introductions
▸ Review of mission, vision, and values
▸ Summary of the organization's history
▸ Organizational structure (board, committees, staff, facilities)
▸ Board culture (in addition to values, etiquette such as degree of formality, expectations regarding discussions and asking questions, etc.)
▸ Key accomplishments in the past few years
▸ Summary of strategic goals
▸ Financial information
▸ Review board expectations and roles

- Assign committees, if not yet done
- Typical board meeting format
- Q and A
- Relevant documents: annual calendar, board roster, previous year-end financial reports, summary of committee commissions, bylaws, conflict of interest policy, annual report

One of your goals is to engage new members as soon as possible, and this is an opportunity to build relationships among board members. While there is no reason to have the entire board attend the orientation, try to arrange a gathering either before or after it to create an opportunity for socializing. For example, if the orientation is held at 4:30 p.m., a cocktail hour could follow. Or a light breakfast could precede it on a Saturday morning. Get creative, and have some fun with it. Your team is making a first impression with new members in regard to how you conduct business.

Mentors

As we know, early engagement results in higher satisfaction and retention of board members. Partnering a new member with a veteran not only shares the responsibility of ensuring a strong connection, but it shortens the learning curve. When making these matches, consider personalities and things the two volunteers may have in common. Are they both parents? Would they be interested in each other's professions? Do they know each other at all? You are looking for a veteran who understands the organization, is a good listener, will follow through, and can relate to the new member. The time commitment is minimal, and *bonus*—you will also be developing leadership skills in the mentor!

I have to share a story about a time when this program didn't work. I thought I was making a good match, connecting a new member with a veteran who served on the same committee. I didn't know the new member very well, and I didn't take the time to ask the volunteer who did know her to give me some background. Long story short, the veteran was a crummy mentor. After the initial introduction, he never contacted her except when they were at the same committee meeting.

I also hadn't created any type of support system to track activity. So three months into the board year, the new member asked me who her mentor was because she'd forgotten. Of course, I don't know if this was her way of letting me know she had a dud or if she really didn't recall. I felt awful. When I contacted the mentor, he thought he was doing a fine job because "I've seen her at two meetings." *Ugh...* he missed the point and I had dropped the ball. I tried to save the match, but the damage was done and the new member was not really interested in connecting with her mentor. So I informally took over the role, and she ended up being a great board member, but not because of our mentor program. If I had applied the Impact Triangle, and thought it through, I would have made a better choice.

A solid mentoring program isn't complicated, but expectations of both parties should be in writing. It encourages contact at least every sixty days, or when a new member misses a meeting. Then the mentor can get in touch to review key points. Additionally, meeting for coffee after the first month or so of service, to see what questions the new member may have, is a nice way to stay connected. The mentor can also encourage the rookie to attend the holiday party, serve as an extra resource during fundraising season, introduce the new member to other board members, and generally strive for a smooth transition. There are a variety of ways to interact as partners, and the relationship should evolve organically based on what seems natural to the individuals.

And, as demonstrated by the example above, you must create a method of monitoring activity, and not just assume the match is working perfectly. A nice way to engage the governance committee is to assign this task to one of the members. Ask for a quarterly report on the matches' activity. Or if it seems as if a new member is only minimally participating, ask the assigned member to bring it to the attention of the committee for a strategy discussion. The more engaged a member is early on, the more likely he or she is to stay involved over time. Watch for the signs.

Committees

Giving serious consideration to which committee is the best match for each member will pay high dividends. I recommend that you let new members know which committees have open seats, outline the goals of each, and say when they meet. Ask the members to indicate their top two choices, then do everything you can to see that they serve on one of their preferred committees. This will be the work team they spend the most time with, so making it meaningful to them matters if you want to retain them. Otherwise it's like going out to recess and being told every week you have to play on the monkey bars, when all you really want to play is four square. Sooner or later you aren't going to want to play at all. Let's make sure our volunteers are playing in an area they enjoy.

Once new members are settled in their committees, take a look at the work plan for the year. Is there a well-thought-out chart of work? A winning practice is having written guidelines for each meeting. So if the marketing committee meets seven times a year, the chart of work will list all seven months with a few bulleted points indicating key topics for each meeting. Examples could be "Review effectiveness of recent ad campaign and make recommendations," or "Hire public relations firm," or "Develop next year's marketing plan." It is the committee chair's job, with support from the staff liaison, to develop the chart of work in alignment with the strategic plan and stay on track throughout the year.

Ensuring that your committee chair is trained and ready to lead is crucial. Have you ever attended a meeting that was disorganized, during which time dragged on and it seemed like you were there forever? Or did the chair cut people off from sharing their perspective? The best-intentioned leaders can still go astray if they have not benefitted from some coaching on your expectations for effective meetings. One of the fastest ways to turn off new volunteers is to waste their time at meetings. Remember—the goal is to engage everyone, build strong relationships, and retain them.

A note on virtual meetings: there are certainly times when they make sense. For example, it may not be practical to meet personally for every meeting if you have a national board; if the agenda is fairly simple, without any major decisions expected; or if there is a need for a meeting to be convened on short notice. I would not recommend a virtual meeting when you know group dynamics will be important to the discussion or when there is a major decision pending. Some people are not as energetic online as in person, and let's face it—it's easy to multitask when no one can see you, and those distractions can take away from meaningful discussion.

Here are some tips for running great committee meetings:

- Send out the meeting agenda a week in advance, so members can be prepared for discussion and action. Also send out any documents that need review—don't waste time in the meeting disseminating them.
- Start on time, no matter what. You will create an expectation of punctuality. If after a few meetings there are several people struggling to arrive on time, discuss changing the time of the meeting.
- Encourage participation from everyone. You have asked them to serve on this committee because you believe they can bring value; the chair needs to hear from each person, and needs to know how to draw people out if they are quiet. If necessary, help the chair learn how to redirect someone who is hijacking the discussion.
- Stick to the agenda (with the most important matters first) and eliminate side conversations or irrelevant discussion.
- Ask staff for clarification and additional information. The committee chair runs the meeting, and the staff person is in a support role. Staff may present information but are not typically key to the decision-making process. A good practice is to have the staff person state his or her perspective when planning the meeting with the chair in order to influence discussion if needed.
- End on time. If there is unfinished business, table it until the next meeting. If it's time sensitive, follow up with a virtual meeting, conference call, or email. If highly critical, ask members if they can stay a few more minutes, but this should not be the norm. Respect their time if you want to retain them.
- Form a subcommittee if a project looks as though it needs deeper research or attention. Assigning two or three people to work offline is certainly acceptable so the entire meeting isn't spent on one topic. A subcommittee should be short term and dissolve when the project is complete.

Committee members will appreciate attending meetings where meaningful work is done and their time and opinions are respected. They will stay engaged and perhaps look for more ways to get involved.

Communication and Accessibility

I think it's important to address this so it doesn't come back to bite you. Intentionally take a look at when, why, and who is communicating with new members. A common mistake is recruiting new members and having them attend the annual meeting in June. Then the board goes dark for almost three months until the first board meeting in September. In the meantime, no one is in touch with the new members, and we expect them to show up for an orientation. Think about relationships and what can be done during the summer to keep members connected. Again, there doesn't need to be a grandiose plan, but you don't want them to think you forgot about them.

So consider something like this: In July the executive director sends out an informative summary about what is going on in the organization over the summer, including some accomplishments, a few data points, and how plans are progressing for the fall event. The goal is to keep the whole board connected. Then perhaps you can hold the new member orientation in August, where the current members get to meet them if they haven't already met. And sometime between the orientation and the first board meeting, perhaps the mentors can have coffee with their matched rookies to see how they are feeling about their experience so far and whether they have any questions.

Board members report to the president of the board. Keeping this in mind, the president will have a keen interest in members' level of satisfaction with their experience. One of the best practices I have seen was in an organization in which the president met with each new board member personally within the first ninety days of their term. There was no agenda except to build the relationship and be available to support their experience. I think this speaks volumes about how valued the new member is to the whole team. Most people like having the undivided attention of the person in charge. It's like knowing the teacher, or coach, or police chief. By the way, this organization had a retention rate every year of 85 to 90 percent of board members who renewed their terms.

I also recommend some extra communication around fundraising time. This could come from the executive director, a mentor, or a member of the development committee. I will talk more about the psychology of fundraising in the next section, but know that if this is the first time a member has been responsible for raising money, it can seem daunting. So spending a little extra time with the rookies will likely be beneficial to both the new members and your organization. When people feel supported, their motivation tends to increase.

A word about how you communicate. Each of you may approach communication differently, but I believe this is a great place to leverage technology. I hope you don't send out hard copies of documents before meetings anymore. They are either emailed or posted online, right? And we know that personal contact is the most effective way to communicate important messages. So phone calls and meetings will always be needed—don't get carried away by thinking all communication can be electronic. But do think about convenience to your volunteers. Meetings notices are a good example. Sending an email with date, time, and key agenda items is good, but sending a calendar invitation that can just be clicked so all the info slips silently into their calendar is even better. And by the time you read this, who knows what new trick will be available that is even more convenient and user-friendly?

Midyear Check

People are social creatures and want to be part of a group, and to feel like they belong. They will be part of a committee, as well as part of the full board. These new members will also be part of the new class of 2017 (example). So let's get this group together, who have in common the honor of being the most recently selected members, and see how they are collectively feeling.

This can be done several ways. I happen to prefer a somewhat casual setting so they feel as comfortable as possible. You can invite them to an informal dinner with a representative from the governance committee, the executive director, and perhaps the board president or another officer. The point is to have some leadership present to show the intended purpose is important to them. Then once everyone is settled in, ask some open-ended questions, such as:

- ► "How are you enjoying your board experience so far?"
- ► "What is going well?"

- "What additional information or resources could we provide?"
- "What concerns you?"
- "What are you looking forward to now?"
- "What surprised you?"
- "What else would you like to share?"

I would encourage you to have a note-taker as well. Obviously, you want to capture key points, but as you keep records of these midyear conversations, it also may be interesting to see if any trends emerge. If you consistently hear concern about unclear committee functions, for instance, then some attention should be paid to structure and coaching of committee chairs. Any relevant information should be utilized to improve systems in the future or address specific issues.

Bonus tip: When you sincerely use members' feedback to adjust things going forward, you gain their respect and trust, and increase their level of engagement.

Social Events

It's that darn social creature thing again. People want to hang out with people they like and with whom they have things in common. So if you are a board president or executive director, I'd encourage you to have a few social events on the calendar. No need to go overboard, and you can certainly delegate the planning. It is nice to entertain members with a little fun, and maybe even weave some recognition into the outing without a big agenda.

So have the holiday party or go to the horse track; if you are near water, have a spring picnic at the lake or a bay cruise. And as brilliant as you are, it makes sense to ask members what they want to do, and when, so you know they can attend. I witnessed a bowling night that I was afraid would flop. Well, we approached it with a silliness that extended to the night of the event, and with various contests (what team could score highest while bowling every other frame with the opposite hand), including coming up with a team name and cheer. It was a blast! You never know.

Leadership Opportunities

I have focused a lot on engaging board members early in their tenure, which is critical. It is also essential to do your best to retain a high level of engagement with veteran board members. Providing leadership opportunities is a wonderful way to do so (see additional information in chapter 17 on succession planning). In addition to officer and committee chair positions, some leadership opportunities aren't so formal or obvious.

Consider some of these options:

► Serve as a mentor
► Lead a project (for example, market research) and report back to the board
► Host an event
► Recruit a fundraising team
► Provide subject matter expertise

It is possible to engage quiet leaders in ways that will be recognized and valued by the team. Board members don't always have to lead from the front, and a strong engagement plan will include several strategies.

Annual Evaluation

I hope you will really pay attention here. You spent a good deal of time thoughtfully selecting new members, planning their orientation, assigning them a mentor, and getting them connected through good committee work, and you have worked hard to keep them feeling valued. You must give them an opportunity to provide honest feedback, anonymously if they wish, to the governance committee. Otherwise, it is like launching a new product or program and then just walking away once it's rolling on its own. You wouldn't do that in any other business, and you can't do that here.

Think about what you want to measure, and develop questions accordingly. It would seem as though questions about the leadership, clarity of roles, commitment to goals, pride in organization, committee work, fundraising, and other board-led projects or events would be in order. Personally, I believe electronic surveys that members can complete at their convenience and anonymously get the best return. Definitely allow for comments on all questions so further explanation can be provided if they wish.

In addition to having individual board members comment on their experience, I would encourage the governance committee to consider an evaluation of individual board members as relevant to team performance. This is not about judging anyone; it is about assessing behavior. Using a matrix with board members' names down the left side and expectations across the top, such as attendance, advocacy, and fund development, is a simple method of assessing performance at a glance. Now, be clear about the purpose. If you have been doing a good job of engaging board members and paying attention, you already will have identified any issues with specific volunteers. The purpose is to notice whether the majority of the board as a whole is meeting annual goals. If at the beginning of the year it was stated that board members were expected to increase the amount of money they raised over the previous year, and the chart shows only 25 percent of members did so, that's good to know. Something needs to be adjusted.

The key is to know what to measure, roll board member performance up into summary metrics, and make informed decisions based on data. You could also measure things such as whether at least half of your board members introduced at least one new person to the organization this year, and whether the board is representative of the community demographically.

Self-evaluations can be utilized also. Typically they are designed to be used only by the individual board member. They can serve as a gut check for members and remind them of expectations. When introduced correctly, this can work well. But be mindful of framing the process in a positive way, so as to avoid defensiveness. It is meant to inspire, not defeat. Engaging volunteers is akin to developing volunteers—you want to provide them with rewarding experiences from which they can learn and grow.

Lastly, as you read these eight engagement strategies, I know what you're thinking, and I can picture the beads of perspiration forming on your forehead and upper lip. You are concerned about all the time this is going to take. First, note that responsibility for these activities is spread among several people, so no one person is getting socked. Second, look at how you are spending your time now. Do you feel like you're spinning your wheels because you are constantly trying to identify new board members? Do you have ineffective meetings because you don't have a quorum? Are you concerned about a lackadaisical attitude from at least some of your board members? You know where I'm going with this. Investing some time up front will save you time in the end. This is working "smart." Plus the additional benefits of a strong board that is inspired to do more, not less, is invaluable.

We're back to that perspective thing. Take a look at what might be stopping you from enthusiastically adopting these concepts. How can you adjust what you believe to start moving forward with commitment and a positive mindset? Now just take the next step forward.

CHAPTER SIXTEEN

GREAT BOARD MEETINGS . . . REALLY

I AM PRETTY SURE that since the beginning of time, many leaders have struggled to run exceptional meetings. I'm not sure why we haven't all been able to get over the hump. There are businesses that have nailed it, so let's start thinking about how to make sustainable change. The process for building a meaningful agenda will become routine, so establish the pattern and don't fall back into old habits. Remember the Impact Triangle. Your mindset will be positive, focused on what is possible and whom you can rely on to assist in the transition. Understanding why productive meetings are important is the first step.

Let's deal with some logistics first.

- **Frequency.** It is abundantly clear to me that boards that meet only three or four times a year are less productive and engaged. It isn't realistic to expect a board to fully participate in meaningful oversight when its members are asked to pay attention only a few times a year. While there is no perfect number of meetings, because every organization and its needs are different, I would suggest meeting at least six times per year.
- **Venue.** The fewer the distractions, the better. This is a business meeting and should be treated as such. If the organization's facilities don't have a large or quiet enough room or the right technology to host the meeting, perhaps a board

member can host it at his or her office, or a donor would underwrite the cost of renting a conference room, or it can be held at the local chamber. Getting it right is directly related to how effective the meeting will be. Ever try to present in a cold, cramped room with no AV? You get the point.

- **Virtual attendance.** Some national boards use this practice frequently. Joining by phone is also common. While that type of participation is better than no participation, understand that it greatly detracts from the goal of engagement. Members aren't present for the social component, they can't feel the energy dynamics (sounds hokey but is a very real nuance of any meeting), and they might not be able to hear all discussion points. I believe this method of participation should be the exception, not the rule.

    When I was working with one organization, over the course of four board meetings a certain member never attended a meeting, but called in each time. She was long tenured on the board and very wise, connected, and in many ways so valuable to the organization. I encouraged leaders to employ some strategies to further engage her. It didn't happen, and she resigned a couple of months later. I'm not suggesting this will always happen, but observing behavior patterns at meetings and beyond allows you to be proactive in terms of engaging members.

- **Food helps.** I hate to have to even mention it, but we are simple creatures. Provide even a simple, healthy snack and people appreciate it. There is a slight chance attendance may improve a bit, too.

- **Time.** I frequently get asked when the best time of day is for a board meeting, and the answer is when your board members can meet. Many meetings are in the morning, others at lunch, and some at night. You will need to consider where most people are commuting from in relationship to the meeting site. But do a quick email survey if you are just starting out or seeing a drop in attendance. The best time is when the majority of your volunteers can attend.

Maintaining Altitude

When board members were recruited, expectations were reviewed and it was made clear that their role is to determine direction and mission, develop strategic initiatives and goals, form policy, be the fiduciary agents of the organization, advocate, fundraise, recruit other board members, attend required meetings to ensure the work gets done, hire and evaluate the executive director, and otherwise provide oversight to the organization.

Now you must hold up your end of the deal. This means you will not encourage or allow volunteers to get involved in the operational minutia. Keep the conversation up at the 15,000-foot level. Honor their commitment and they will continue to serve. As soon as they feel their time is wasted on items that don't require their expertise, they will start to check out.

Some volunteers may want to slip down into the weeds because they have a particular interest in that part of the business. They may want to discuss details of a specific program, or they may try to get involved in personnel decisions. But staff will manage those areas, and if the board members have relevant questions, they are better handled outside the boardroom. Board meetings are not going to spend time on details like what color tile is best for the lobby.

A Skilled President

Additionally, if meetings are poorly run by a president who lacks experience or dominates the meeting, this could be disastrous for your team. Watch attendance dwindle. Have you ever been in a meeting where one person starts debating every single point? It takes a special skill to redirect the discussion to the agenda. If leadership is behind the curve here, I would recommend taking quick action before the next meeting. The executive director can provide coaching tips on how to manage a derailed discussion while still honoring various perspectives.

As part of the succession planning process (see chapter 17) you will outline the list of skills and experience needed for a board president. Running good meetings is one of them, and to do so takes leadership, keen observation and awareness skills, and the technical ability to manage any situation. It is also important that the board respects their leader.

A Strong Agenda

If the agenda is weak, without any significant decisions to be made or meaningful discussion items, volunteers will start to wonder why you need them. All fluff is not a winning practice. Giving committee reports when minutes have been made available is a another quick way to impending doom. Did you catch that? Please, I'm begging you, do *not* have committees report unless there is a recommendation that needs action. Adults can read minutes—and shame on them if they don't. It is, however, certainly appropriate to allow time for questions regarding the minutes that were distributed in advance.

Now that I have touched on what *not* to do when preparing an agenda, here are some proven steps to take to keep your meetings meaningful and infused with energy. I know this sounds very elementary, but if enough thought was put into planning agendas, we would not need to talk about it. I suggest that the executive director and board president discuss what the main objectives are for the meeting. Periodically asking the opinion of other key members on the board is also a great idea. They will be in the audience—what do they feel is critical to the organization now? And what is the best way to address it?

Advanced tip: When having this discussion, look out several months. There may be some critical topics coming up that require allocation of time on a series of agendas, plus you don't want to get caught up in too much short-term thinking and miss an opportunity to impact a key strategy. A good practice is to report on the strategic plan at least quarterly; then you will ensure the big picture is being addressed.

This conversation will result in identification of an overarching goal for the specific meeting, and from there you can plan accordingly. If it is just prior to the annual campaign, you may wish to do some brainstorming on how to identify new prospects, ask for recommitment to the development strategies, or ask a few members to tell their story about why they choose to advocate for this organization in an effort to further inspire others.

Allow for Socialization

I just want to add a quick a reminder that your board members find their relationships with the rest of the team to be valuable. So create space and time for some relationship building. Whether it's just before or after the meeting doesn't matter. But don't underestimate the importance of this time for them. And if you are engaging the board well, they may even have some of the organization's business to discuss with their volunteer peers.

Create a Culture of Inquiry

There was a time as an executive director when I was in a board meeting and no one ever said a word except the board president, and me when it was time to give my report. It was torture, and quite frankly embarrassing. And it motivated me to change how meetings were run. We didn't need a bunch of puppets sitting there nodding their heads. These were bright, talented volunteers who were looking to us for direction on how best to utilize their gifts. And we were ignoring them. How disrespectful! I knew what I really wanted was to have them ask questions, challenge assumptions, and bring forth new ideas. But for some reason, they didn't feel inspired to do so, or didn't realize this would be welcome.

If you find yourself in a similar situation, try some of these tips. At the next meeting, as volunteers arrive, hand them an index card and ask them to write down one thing they either don't understand or would like to see changed about the organization. You will need to be gently firm, because a few folks may want to skirt the activity. But convince them to trust you, and reassure them that their responses are anonymous. Tell them you are looking for new ideas.

Then you can do a couple of things, depending on what gets written down. Before the meeting starts, glance through the cards and pick out a response that could be discussed in ten to fifteen minutes. Then at a predetermined time on the agenda, the president will read each card to the board, take them all seriously, and thank members for taking a moment to jot down what is on their mind. You can let them know you will give consideration to each item, and then start discussion on the one topic you chose out of the group.

I understand this might be out of your comfort zone, so check your mindset. Your goal is to engage the board and enter into meaningful dialogue to which everyone can contribute. If you frame it well, and set the tone by letting members know you are very interested in their perspective, you will achieve your goal. There may be unfinished business, which is fine, because you got them talking. And then it's what you do with the points made during the discussion that matters most.

I have seen boards literally transform when they adopt a culture of inquiry. Asking questions is a good thing—it means members care and are engaged. When you ensure that everyone is heard, has the opportunity to learn, and knows his or her opinion matters, it is very powerful.

Include Generative Discussions

As this culture is further developed, you can then intentionally identify when discussions will be *fiduciary* (primarily focused on legal and financial matters, oversight of operations, and allocation of resources), *strategic* (looking at the business model, market share, competitive advantage, and the best way to get to the next goal), or *generative* (creatively framing issues, usually moving away from a logic model, encouraging healthy debate versus quick consensus). These are the three types of governance, and each has its place. The most successful organizations, ones with strong boards, are actively participating in generative discussions. In order for this to work well, the group must be diverse.

Generative discussions gather the collective wisdom of the group. This builds trust because of the open dialogue that challenges assumptions or beliefs. I once had an executive director say that she didn't have any critical issues or challenges to talk about. Nice, but that probably meant there were some hidden issues, or opportunities were getting missed.

The tricky part about this type of conversation is that it isn't designed to solve the problem, but rather to ask the question creatively and extract ideas. For most of us, it's counterintuitive to not be focused on the solution. If you are wondering on what issues to frame questions, watch for tension, confusion, silence, or ambiguity during interactions. Perhaps somewhere in there is an underlying issue to be further explored.

Depending on your organization, here are some possible questions to consider when you wish to have a generative discussion. I have compiled this list from a variety of sources.

▶ What if we merged with another organization with a similar mission? Would we be stronger?

- If we could be number one on any list, what list would it be?
- What would happen if we stopped existing?
- What has been the biggest challenge we've faced, and what did we learn?
- The mayor is giving a press conference about us at 5 p.m.—what will she say?
- What's the biggest gap between what we claim to do and what we actually do?

Generative discussions aren't meant to be time-fillers, but instead hearty discussions about something of importance to the organization. You may not even know exactly what you are trying to get at, but the dialogue can stimulate great ideas that might lead toward important awareness and strategies. If you break the team into smaller groups for table discussions, that can lend itself to a higher level of participation. Then ask each group to report a summary back to the larger group.

Include Mission Moments

When boards are operating well, it's actually common to hear whispers like, "I'm not really clear on what type of services and programs we offer." When boards are focused at a high level, they may miss out on a great new program that came along, because they are busy recruiting members or identifying new revenue streams. Of course, you don't want that to be the case, because the very information they are missing is the information they can use to help support the goals they are striving to reach. In addition, hearing actual examples of impact is very inspiring.

So consider spending a few minutes at each meeting showing how the mission is at work.

- You can invite a beneficiary of your services to share his or her story.
- You can ask staff to share a program overview focused on how a critical need is being met.
- You can have a major donor visit to speak about why he or she invests in the organization.

There are many ways to do this, and the time spent on reminding board members why they joined in the first place will reignite their passion.

Respect Time

Again, this may seem like common sense, but I've seen the brightest people fall victim to the never-ending meeting. Anything more than ninety minutes is ineffective, in my opinion, and I've attended hundreds of board meetings with many different organizations. My favorite misstep is when a recommendation is made, the board approves it, but discussion continues afterward for ten more minutes. Sometimes it's because a few dissenters want to drive their point home, or maybe someone was reluctant to speak up and now has a thought. But it's not okay. The vote was taken, so move on to the next agenda item.

Here are some things to keep in mind:

▸ Put the most important items at the top of the agenda so you are sure to get to them.

▸ Include a consent agenda where appropriate, having sent those items to members in advance (check the rules on consent agenda in your bylaws for guidance).

▸ Time out the agenda in advance so there are no surprises. It's easier to stick to a plan when you have one.

▸ Follow Robert's Rules of Order. This will help things move in an organized fashion and ensure you are following a solid decision-making process.

▸ Remember what I said about starting and ending committee meetings on time? Same applies here. Set the expectation, and honor their time.

Great board meetings will focus on strategy, report on impact measurements, encourage discussion, ensure learning occurs, and provide opportunity for building relationships among members. The work is critically important to the community, so getting it right matters.

Sample Agenda

(Social time immediately preceding or following)
1. Call to Order
2. Consent Agenda Items – action required
3. President's Report (overview of key organizational items)
4. Finance Committee: Budget recommendations and action required

5. Strategic Plan Progress (include an impact report)
6. Board Discussion Item – addressing the challenge of facility restrictions
7. Mission Moment – program highlight
8. Development Committee – fundraising plan needs
9. Executive Director report (operations update; ask for input/ideas)
10. New ideas, other business
11. Adjourn

Your ability to employ the Impact Triangle in order to conduct engaging meetings will significantly affect results. Your meetings will be interesting, your team members will interact with each other, and these winning practices will lead to improved results. Be bold and try new things! To run meaningful meetings is to keep volunteers engaged and maintain a high retention rate, which ultimately serves the community well.

CHAPTER SEVENTEEN

SUCCESSION PLANNING

HAVE YOU HAD IT HAPPEN? You get the call and the board president tells you she's moving to accept a new position. Next month. Campaign kicks off in six weeks. There is no one who could come close to stepping up and leading well. *Uh-oh.* Your organization's volunteer leadership team is designed to be temporary. Therefore, planning to develop new leaders is not only sound business, but a critical step in creating stability.

Unlike strategic planning, which most people know they should but aren't motivated to do, succession planning is very often just overlooked. Succession planning refers to the intentional process of identifying and developing people with the potential and interest to fill key leadership positions in the organization. I have also heard it referred to as "replacement planning," but I believe it's more than that. Most organizations see the value in a strong talent-focused volunteer development program at all levels.

There are several reasons for investing in a strategic process for succession:

- ▶ Avoid uncertainty and instability
- ▶ Provide professional and personal growth opportunities
- ▶ Retain talented individuals

- Ensure continued progress toward goals
- Identify competency gaps among the team
- Provide leadership continuity
- Be more nimble and flexible to manage adversity
- Energize and build excitement for the future

Your board members are certainly loyal and committed to advancing the mission, and they make sacrifices to do so, but typically there are term limits. This means they are temporary members of the team, which is an even stronger argument for intentional succession planning.

Even if you are leading a new organization and just building the board, this is a great time to carefully consider whom to recruit. Keep an eye out for future leaders. Since you know the officers and committee chairs will be rotating out of those positions, what are you doing to prepare for the transition?

Who and How?

Before the work can start, there needs to be support of this type of planning from the president, executive director, and board as a whole. If the board hasn't discussed the topic lately, put it on a board meeting agenda and start the discussion. The idea will likely resonate with business people, especially if they supervise employees, since this is a regular practice in the corporate sector. Once the board understands the benefits and agrees to move forward with the planning process, the real work can start.

Succession planning is a function of the governance/board development committee. This group is responsible for recruiting, retaining, and recognizing board members. If you don't have such a committee, please create one.

When done well, their annual work plan is one of the meatiest and most important functions in the organization. Since this committee is identifying qualified candidates for the board, they are best positioned to guide the succession planning effort. Among other things, they are looking for leadership skills when vetting nominees.

What Do You Need?

In order to identify the right people for the right spots, you must understand what you need. First, develop a leadership profile for each position that aligns with your strategic goals. I might suggest outlining a matrix, similar to the one for assessing board composition, but this is for a different purpose, so look at it with a different perspective. This process relates to lining up the leaders who will be in key positions to set the tone and direction of your organization. For example, you might have four officer positions—president, vice president, treasurer, and secretary—and four standing committee chairs. These eight positions should have a simple, yet thoughtful, list of criteria you are looking for in a volunteer leader.

I think it's also important to focus on experience within the organization. I wouldn't want a president elected who hadn't served as a committee chair, at least, and/or as the annual campaign chair. And if you have a capital campaign coming up, you will need your president to be well known and respected in the community, with demonstrated leadership skills, in order to persevere throughout the campaign. Remember, these traits should be linked to the organizational goals of your business.

Some other competencies, attributes, or experience examples include:

- Able to manage or initiate change
- Motivated toward results
- Works well with diverse groups of people
- Sound decision-maker
- Financially astute
- Manages conflict
- Understands volunteer dynamics
- Leads teams
- Promotes inclusion
- Strong communicator/listener
- Chaired at least one committee or project

These lists can get quite long, so they may take a few iterations, and whittling down activities to arrive at the most desired traits. I'd stick to no more than eight for each position, and there could be some overlap. I would suggest one characteristic that is essential for any leadership role is the desire to learn and be open to personal growth and development. Know-it-alls and stick-in-the-muds need not apply.

Do You Have What You Need?

This is a big question, because there are two powerful components to it. The first part is assessing whether there are people on the board who meet the criteria outlined for the key leadership positions. How will you assess that? Again, this is a responsibility of the board development committee. By the way, I believe it's brilliant to have the president elect as a member of this committee—this person will lead the next group of leaders, so let's get his or her perspective and involvement in the decisions.

Back to assessing—for volunteers, this process is fairly subjective. However, asking key questions is important.

- ► How did they perform in a recent leadership role?
- ► Have they demonstrated the qualities identified as critical for the position?
- ► How are they perceived by other board members?
- ► Do they work well with staff?

You may want to draft a short questionnaire that the committee completes individually, and then compare responses. How you conduct this step is less important than that it gets done, and in an honest way that includes several people so no single opinion sways the decision.

Next, you need to determine whether the potential leader is interested in assuming this key role. Great leaders may politely decline for various reasons. Sometimes it's a lack of confidence, sometimes they truly aren't interested, sometimes they have too many competing priorities and just can't commit—another time might be better. And trust me, trying to convince someone to step into a key role he or she doesn't want is asking for trouble. I know from experience.

For two years I had asked the same fabulous gentleman to step up and chair a committee—he was so well qualified! He turned me down both times, but I'm persistent. The third year, I wore him down and he reluctantly said yes. All year he went through the motions, but he was not motivated. How stupid of me! I should have really listened. But no. So instead we had a great group of volunteers who had a lackluster time at best that year. *Ugh!* Lesson learned: We can't *make* people want to do something.

Have you run into the opposite problem yet? Someone keeps raising her hand and saying, "Pick me!", though you know she isn't really equipped for the position. This can get awkward, but again, stick to the process and choose well. Usually, there is a place in the organization that matches a volunteer's skill set, especially if you've done a good job recruiting board members. Let people know what criteria and experience you're looking for, either for the position they want or another, and start working with them to develop those areas. Motivated volunteers are a precious commodity, and I would encourage you to honor them.

Developing Through the Gap

Usually, strong candidates don't possess all the desired traits. No need to panic. This is where the very meaningful art of developing board members comes into play. Let's say you have identified a candidate to chair the development committee, but he is missing significant experience with the annual campaign. It is up to you to provide that opportunity to best prepare him for a bigger role. Do *not* just skip it and decide the person is so great, he will just figure things out. That's a disservice to him and the organization. You want to position people for success in the best possible way. Furthermore, the criteria were developed for this very reason; stick to them or you will soon realize you have a diluted leadership team, incapable of meeting expectations for the organization.

Since you have the profile of an ideal candidate, share it with interested board members and get their perspective. They may reveal they have experience in other organizations that you were not aware of, or they may show a lack of confidence in a different area of which you were not aware. However that conversation goes, it's in the next steps where the real opportunity lies. Now do something to close any gaps. There is more information about how adults learn in the staff development section of this book (see chapter 29), but for now, let's remember that we learn best by doing.

It's up to the executive director and president of the board to create learning opportunities for these folks waiting in the wings. Some things may be best done individually, while for other needs, a group situation is appropriate. A good example of this is to conduct a committee chair workshop before the board year begins. Invite current chairs (some will be veterans and others will be first-timers) as well as vice chairs (or however you identify the next chairs in line). Agenda items can include how to build an agenda, the role of staff in committees, best practices for running effective meetings, etc. So even though they aren't leading a committee this year, they will get introduced to the role early. Then throughout the year, they will be observing the chair and be encouraged to ask questions between meetings.

The above scenario is also a great development opportunity for the current committee chair, who will mentor and coach the incoming chair before that person steps into the new position. The veteran can fill the incoming chair in on the nuances of dealing with different personalities; outline why he or she chose to have a subcommittee work on a project offline; and explain the relationship with the board chair, to which the committee chair reports, among other things. Imagine how great it would have been if in every new role you undertook, there was someone there to help prepare you!

In addition to this type of structured training and mentoring, real experiential opportunities are very effective in supporting the learning process. Perhaps the vice chair can lead the subcommittee for a specific project before taking on the committee chair role. This gives experience in leading teams, organizing agendas, and managing different perspectives. If a person needs more fundraising experience before leading the board, provide him or her the chance to lead a major section of the annual campaign, coordinate an event, or visit a major donor.

You can also fill in the gaps by providing resources, such as books and webinars. Have you ever thought about introducing an upcoming leader to leaders of other organizations? Not only is this a networking opportunity, but an outside perspective on what it takes to lead can be eye-opening and bring a deeper understanding of the position. Look for creative ways to fill in the gaps for your inspired volunteers.

Oh yeah, and remember to budget for this important process!

I want to also mention the difference in generations and expectations, as this will affect your style of volunteer development. If we're honest, many established boards are composed of wonderful volunteers who are mostly over forty years old. Now don't start berating me! I understand it's not fair to group, and I understand this isn't true everywhere. But it is in a lot of places. So stay with me for a minute.

Different generations have different needs, and this is a great opportunity to point out that your concern isn't only about the organization's needs, but also about the needs of the people you are grooming.

Perhaps they prefer a more collaborative culture. Are you prepared to shift the way things are done? They may point out that there is less need for hierarchy, or a simple way to use technology more effectively when communicating. Think about this—will you flex with the changing times in order to be able to attract and keep strong leaders, even when it means doing things differently? If not, the dynamic younger leaders may go elsewhere and you will be left with a missed opportunity.

Board members who are asked to lead, and who are provided with opportunities to build commitment and capacity, feel valued. Being part of a leadership team typically leads to a higher level of engagement. This means the whole community benefits, because now these people will stay involved with the organization longer. And a strong leadership team with the right mindset, people, and skills is a powerful force.

Is It Working?

When you do all this work to encourage individual advancement and empower the human capital in your organization, one essential component of the plan is to step back and evaluate whether it's working. Initially, you set some goals to keep moving your organization forward through succession planning. How are you measuring results?

▸ Did the training and development work?
▸ Did you identify the right folks?
▸ Do you need to adjust the leadership profile?

Again, outline some key questions around the metrics that matter, and rate the process. And please remember that it's not all about you; ask the volunteer leaders whether they are pleased with the process and role they are filling. Then take the results of your evaluation and adjust the plan. Being adaptive to ensure best results is good business.

Operationalize It

Great idea, good plan—and it will never get done unless you incorporate it into how you do business. So look at how you already have things set up, and determine how this plan can get folded into your normal work. By now I'm hoping you have written annual work plans for committees. I would recommend adding these succession planning steps to your board development committee calendar.

The executive director, with support from the president, is responsible for managing the volunteers. So there needs to be an accountability component. A simple performance standard stating that the committees are reaching the outlined goals could work, with emphasis on succession planning the first year or two it's implemented.

By the way, when you first create a succession plan, if you look around and don't have a deep bench of leaders waiting to be placed in key positions, don't worry too much. It's what you do next that matters. It will usually take a year or two to get well positioned; be sure to focus on recruiting new board members with this need in mind and you will be ahead of the curve.

Here is an example of how you might work succession planning into the board calendar if your board year gets rolling in July.

- ▶ Executive director identifies what leadership positions will be open eighteen months in advance.
- ▶ Board development committee evaluates the succession plan from the previous year – January.
- ▶ President and committee chairs are asked to submit names of potential successors (any officer positions, too) in February the year before vacant; goal is to stagger the number rotating off each year.

- Potential leaders are identified by a small team (board president, past president, vice presidents, executive director) – by March.
- Potential leaders are contacted and level of interest determined (president) - April.
- Development plans are created for these potential leaders, as needed (board development committee and executive director) – July each year.
- New leaders are coached and mentored for one year, and then transitioned into role August of the next year.
- These dedicated volunteers are encouraged and recognized – year round!

Congratulations! You have taken the first steps. I truly believe that succession planning is one of the most important strategies that can make or break an organization. Without it, the same leaders continue to overstay their tenure, and they burn out. They may leave, and then the organization, hence the community, starts to suffer. Or it's like a revolving door with key positions, and the organization is constantly in a transition phase with very slow progress toward strategic initiatives.

Either way, a good plan will remove many of these issues and let you begin to work wisely toward developing board members, increasing retention, and achieving amazing results. Find the right mindset and focus clearly, put the right people in place, and utilize best practices to implement the plan. You will end up accelerating your impact.

CHAPTER EIGHTEEN

CELEBRATING!

YOU HAVE THE HONOR of working with some very special people. They pour their hearts into their volunteer work. It would be easy to keep chugging away toward the next priority, the next goal to achieve. There is always something more to do, right? Well, let's make sure that recognizing your board members is high on the list of things to do. This is the fun part, so be sure to celebrate!

When you think of the Impact Triangle, the mindset part of recognition is probably not too much of a challenge. I think most of us inherently understand that it feels good to get a pat on the back. And we want to be sure our volunteers know we appreciate them. The board development committee will create a simple plan for this, which can be dropped right into the annual calendar of their work. Regardless of your role in the organization, offer up suggestions. Think about how you would like to be recognized, and share your ideas.

Recognition can serve as a significant motivator; it's something that reenergizes board members and factors into their level of satisfaction. It validates that the work they have contributed is valued. Recognition can keep them more engaged, and therefore increase retention. However, the recognition must be sincere and specific to their effort. It is never acceptable to use recognition as a type of manipulation to keep someone involved.

One point to note is that different people like to be acknowledged in various ways. So as you are planning to thank someone, consider that the person may have something completely different in mind. This holds true for groups as well. If you plan to recognize a committee, or even the whole board, give some thought to what will be best received. There are clear benchmarks for your team that deserve recognition—shoot, take the whole board out for a happy hour or to a baseball game when you blow past a campaign goal or surpass a particularly challenging goal in your strategic plan!

When offering individual recognition, think about the personality and style of the recipient. If people are highly social and like being around others, some type of public recognition is appropriate. These are the folks whooping it up on the dance floor during your annual gala. Others may be more reserved and will just appreciate a note, or a discreet thank you. Some even think recognition is unnecessary because they are simply doing what is expected, and the intrinsic reward is enough. Some volunteers are motivated by the prestige of the recognition, so use fancy words or titles like "VIP," or superlatives such as "extraordinary." You will have an idea about what type of recognition is best, because you have gotten to know these folks well. Right?

There are many ways to show appreciation. Here are ten ways that I think are unique or clever:

▶ Create a "President's Award," which is given yearly by the board president to the member of the board who has done exemplary work.

▶ For the board member who is always putting out fires, buy and present him or her with a real firefighter's hat engraved with appropriate accolades. Present several different hats to the board member who wears many hats.

▶ When beginning the strategic planning process, give everyone involved a calculator, ruler, or abacus that says "Everyone counts when it comes to (state your mission or organization's name)." This acknowledges participation, even if in a very minor way.

▶ For your annual meeting or board retreat, use Photoshop to put your board members' group photo on a Wheaties box. What an amazing team!

- Have a "bright idea" award for the board members with the most innovative idea that has gotten some traction. You might want to give out a lamp or a supply of light bulbs (keeping energy conservation in mind, of course).
- To celebrate an achievement, send an email message with an appropriate mp3 song as an attachment, such as "She Works Hard for Her Money," "Taking Care of Business," or "The Hallelujah Chorus."
- Give board members Post-it notes or note pads with your logo, phone number, and website.
- At the end of a long board meeting or retreat, hire a massage therapist to do chair massages.
- Give all of your board members lottery tickets with the note "Our clients (or members) don't have to take a chance on their future with you on our board."
- Surprise a particularly industrious board member by having the member's car washed and detailed during a meeting.

As you can see, some of these things may be more public than others, or have a certain tone of lightheartedness to them. Again, knowing how to customize your appreciation to the individual is important. Keep timing in mind also—if you wait until a board meeting that is three months away to thank someone, the meaning may be diminished. Timely and sincere gratitude is the best kind, and it plays a key role in building a strong board.

Summary of Key Points

1. The relationship between executive director and board president is an interesting dynamic. To build a strong relationship, frame expectations early, ask each other questions, and listen to understand how the other person would like you to work together. Get to know and trust each other.

2. Volunteers want to help your organization. Don't assume otherwise. Equip them and hold them accountable—they may surprise you. Mutually supportive relationships bring out the best in both people.

3. Identify some champions, who understand the goal and appreciate the process toward change, to work alongside you and help motivate the rest of the board.

4. The governance committee facilitates the recruitment process, with key roles being played by the executive director and president of the board.

5. The six steps to successful recruitment are assessing current board composition and outlining needs, identifying potential candidates, formally nominating candidates, vetting the nominees against needs, interviewing the top candidates, then selecting and approving.

6. Recruiting younger board members isn't that mysterious—use the same process, be strategic about where to find them, get to know them, and find out what they need and want in order to have a good experience. Diversity is good; appreciate and welcome it.

7. The board is responsible for setting the organization's strategic direction, for ensuring the mission and purpose is served, and for the financial health of the organization.

8. Build trust early by clearly outlining board member expectations in a written agreement. List the expectations related to participation, investing, legal and fiduciary responsibilities, advocacy in the community, and other areas, and require each new member to sign it.

9. The most important factor in board performance is engagement, and it is the executive director's responsibility to identify effective strategies for each member so everyone feels valued. In addition, these steps will increase your board retention: conduct a meaningful orientation, assign

mentors to new members, assign them to appropriate committees (then run great meetings), communicate regularly and effectively, conduct a midyear check-in, create opportunities for socializing, and administer an annual board evaluation.

10. Conducting productive and engaging board meetings is an art, requiring careful preparation and an understanding that the board is tasked with the high-level oversight of the organization—not the operational details. Ensure the best people are in leadership positions.

11. Great meetings include these components: attention to logistics, a carefully planned agenda, social time, mission moments, consent agenda items where appropriate, a culture of inquiry, meaningful generative discussions, a clear process for decision-making, and respect for time.

12. Succession planning is essential for ongoing stability in the organization. Things to consider include clarifying the desired leadership profile for each position, assessing who may possess the desired traits and be interested in advancement, creating a plan to best develop the successor for the position, and evaluating the process afterward to ensure continuous improvement.

13. Recognizing board members is an important step in building strong boards and needs to be customized for the individual or team.

Action Steps

Review your board development plan to determine what areas could benefit from some retooling. Pay particular attention to recruitment, retention, and succession planning.

Share those thoughts with the board development/governance committee, and outline strategies with a timeline for execution.

Encourage the executive director and board president to communicate regularly, and focus on board engagement. Plans are irrelevant without a committed team.

PART FOUR

APPLYING THE IMPACT TRIANGLE TO FUND DEVELOPMENT

4

CHAPTER NINETEEN

EARNED REVENUE AND SOCIAL ENTERPRISE

AS I LOOK AT THE STATE of nonprofits today and how current trends may affect the long term, I am concerned about a few things. At the top of my list is the mix of revenue sources for social organizations. On one hand, I can understand why you are so focused on philanthropic dollars. It's what you have always done, and you must raise funds as part of your charitable mission. But there is no reason to be so dependent on fundraising. Wouldn't it be nice to have unrestricted and renewable revenue to support the charitable mission? So let's explore the notion further and look at social enterprise.

Fund development includes earned revenue—that means some type of fee for service. And yet, many organizations reflect more than half of their operating dollars from donations and grants. No wonder you are feeling such pressure! Look at this remarkable example of what is being called social entrepreneurship; I just call it smart business, but you will see what I mean.

Go to your closest device—laptop, tablet, phone, or anything with internet access—and search for DePaul Industries in Oregon. In addition to information about their company, look for the "Additional Materials" tab and peruse the 2012–2016 strategic plan. They have received awards for their business model and for being one of the best places to work. They have been around since the

1970s, and their vision is "To change the landscape of employment for people with disabilities." Their mission is "To help people with disabilities have the opportunity to work."

DePaul Industries realized in the 1980s that their organization would have to evolve in order to remain viable. They derived about two-thirds of their revenue from government grants, which was not going to be sustainable. So they looked hard at the double bottom line and embraced the idea of using business to drive social good. As you will see, they found wonderful ways to continue to advance their mission and provide staffing, manufacturing, and security services to the community. For example, they are charging their customers for staffing services and reinvesting that revenue stream into the organization to support training and more. By being strategic about how they scale their programs, they have increased earned revenue dramatically while providing more opportunities for people with disabilities.

This may be a shift in thinking for many organizations in the social sector. You may have the perspective that good works should be free. And indeed, in many cases, the beneficiaries of critically needed programs are not in a position to pay for services. But what if you looked at it a little differently? What if you looked at the assets (facilities, products, programs, services) you already possess and started thinking about how you could leverage a different type of revenue, and in turn, possibly a stronger ROI in terms of social impact, while reducing the need for donated funds?

I recently learned of an organization in San Diego called Dreams for Change. Their mission is "To decrease hardships faced by low to moderate income families and individuals by providing support and transition through advocacy, innovative programs and services focusing on homelessness, employment, education and asset building." They are innovative and inspiring! In an effort to serve healthy meals to the homeless, they got into the food truck business. After a long learning curve and establishing essential relationships, they have been able to get approval to accept food stamps at their trucks. Impressive! They have stayed true to their values, and are serving in a bold way while strengthening their bottom lines. Additionally, they serve meals to customers with cash, which contributes to their sustainability.

In keeping with the Impact Triangle philosophy, more heads are better than one. I would recommend looking for some champions and doing some brainstorming. When it looks like there may be some possibilities to explore, pull the team together and see what might come out of a strategy session. I would encourage you to invite someone who is knowledgeable about the social enterprise model to join your conversation. You are looking for diverse thinking to get the most out of the discussion.

Here are some questions to consider:

- What are we providing at no cost that could become a revenue stream?
- What other assets, services, or execution advantages could we "sell"?
- How could we expand these areas of the organization?
- What is the level of demand for these assets/services?
- Where are opportunities to partner with another organization?
- How can we create a new—and relevant—product arm of the business?
- Are these new business ideas consistent with our mission and culture?
- Are we moving outside the rules of unrelated business income?

Some ideas that come forth might relate to repurposing facility space (could you rent out some rooms to other organizations for gatherings, or even long term?), utilizing your staff experts to train others or provide consulting, selling merchandise, or creating an online membership that provides items of interest or VIP opportunities to members.

Other Enterprise Models

For-profit businesses have been engaging in socially conscious endeavors for decades. I attended a TedX talk by Jon Carder, the founder of MOGL. He is very committed to fighting hunger in the United States and has created a meal-for-a-meal program so that when diners use their technology and spend at least $20 for a meal at a participating restaurant, MOGL donates a meal to Feeding America. Check out their work at www.mogl.com and see a great example of how a for-profit enterprise is actively supporting charitable organizations, and making a profit while doing it. That nexus between social purpose and business is becoming increasingly powerful. How can you get in the game?

There are other for-profit companies that simply distribute a portion of their profits to charitable organizations. TOMS Shoes is one of the most popular—their One to One giving program donates shoes and glasses to over fifty countries. Check out www.toms.com for their latest giving report.

I have not yet jumped on the bandwagon of the venture-capital type of investors who will turn around your struggling nonprofit and take a percent of revenue generated from the change. I feel a conflict there when the mission calls for services that benefit the public. However, that debate is for another time, and it will be exciting to see how things evolve.

There are also social impact bonds, where investors provide capital, the nonprofit organization does their good work, and the government pays the investors back if the goal is achieved. The premise is that innovative programs can reduce costs to the public via prevention strategies, and the performance-based investments replace start-up funding that may be hard to secure. Typically, an intermediate organization coordinates the project. Investors, organizations, and the community all benefit, and the government is released from having to consider addressing the need directly.

Corporate Social Responsibility

Let's take a look at CSR as it relates to support of the social sector. According to www.investopedia.com, CSR is "corporate initiative to assess and take responsibility for the company's effects on the environment and impact on social welfare." So keeping in mind that nonprofits are organizations with social missions, there is definitely opportunity here, and I wonder if you are proactively doing all you can to support these corporate initiatives. Are you joining forces with companies in public-private partnerships to expand your service to the community?

It's been refreshing to see corporations become more sophisticated in their social responsibility work in the past decade. And you can usually see which ones are just going through the motions by simply throwing money at a cause, or promoting their social commitment by using a tagline without any substance behind it, so don't be fooled. The ones who are genuinely committed realize the benefits to their company and employees, as well as to the greater good.

Net Impact is a San Francisco–based nonprofit with more than three hundred chapters worldwide. They provide support, connections, and practical advice to help people in all sectors and job functions create a more just and sustainable future. In 2012 they conducted a survey in conjunction with other research partners and funders and wrote the "Talent Report: What Workers Want in 2012." It focused on employee engagement and factors that affect satisfaction. This study reveals that employees who say they have the opportunity to make a direct social and environmental impact through their job report higher satisfaction levels than those who don't.

In their study, over half of the student population (defined as graduating university students) would take a 15 percent pay cut to "work for an organization whose values are like my own." Other statistics related to why they would consider a pay cut are:

45% for a job that makes a social or environmental impact
35% to work for a company committed to CSR
58% to work for an organization with values like my own
To see the full report, go to www.netimpact.org/whatworkerswant.

There are certainly other factors that contribute to employee satisfaction, such as opportunities for advancement, relationship with the boss, and job flexibility. But what this study confirms for us is that more young workers will lean toward accepting employment at companies that are able to walk the talk in terms of the broader mission for society.

Additionally, 90 percent of human resource professionals say that pro bono volunteering is an effective way to develop leadership skills. Volunteering can also develop soft skills such as problem solving, mentoring, and communications, that are instrumental in a business environment, according to Ryan Scott, "How Corporate Volunteer Programs Increase Employee Engagement" (Corporate Philanthropy and Volunteering Blog, Feb. 16, 2012).

So where is the opportunity for you? Let's think strategically and creatively about this. We know that individuals give money, not corporations. Whom do you already partner with, or know within businesses? How are you cultivating those relationships? Do they know your future plans to serve the community? Have you visited them lately to hand deliver an invitation to your upcoming event? Have you asked if they would give you a little space in their company e-newsletter, or at least a link to your website? Do you know how many of their employees are in your database and already have a connection to your organization? Can you provide a workshop with other nonprofits for employees on needs in the community? Do their employees know about the opportunities to volunteer within your organization?

Now I know that navigating these waters can be a little tricky, because some companies don't want to give you direct access to their employees. They may be supporting many organizations and are reluctant to be perceived as showing favoritism. So help them sort through that—this is about the employees and what they want. You can be part of their solution (another relationship-building strategy, by the way). So try to turn that mindset around—have you sat with the decision-makers recently and asked them to weigh in on a key project or initiative that will make sustainable change in the community? If these companies are planning to be around for a while, they want to be part of that too, because their employees are expecting them to be involved. The combined impact could be very powerful.

As you reassess your strategic initiatives, consider employees in other companies who are inspired by your work. CSR is an opportunity with massive potential, even if you just look at it as a numbers game. You will reach far more people by utilizing the reach of your corporate partners than you could ever do with just your team. And as you know, strong relationships lead to volunteers, donors, employees, participants, and vendors. Our younger generations are demanding a social perspective. So jump in the game and make the rules, guide the work, and achieve amazing results.

You may have heard of for-profit benefit corporations that are committed to making a positive impact on society and the environment. They adhere to a set of standards and are required to publish an annual benefit report. More states are adopting this corporate structure as another option now. The trend toward increased CSR is clear.

Strengthening your revenue sources can be fun! There is also a lot to consider, and when you determine what direction makes the most sense for your organization, be sure to consult experts and lawyers to outline any parameters that you might not know exist. Then line up best practices and pilot some avenues of work toward increased sustainability.

The bottom line, so to speak, is to shift your perspective if necessary to position your organization for the most success by having a diversified revenue mix. Funders expect you to run a strong business, using a sound business model, and will support the organizations that can prove they are working toward this goal.

CHAPTER TWENTY

THE SCARY F WORD—FUNDRAISING

LET'S CLARIFY A DEFINITION here: fund development relates to all aspects of resource development. All revenue streams—fee for service, grants, and fundraising activities—are included. Fundraising refers to activities such as special events, individual giving campaigns, crowd funding, planned giving, grants, direct mail, capital campaigns, etc. In this chapter we are focusing on fundraising activities. We are striving for a culture of philanthropy.

This word *fundraising* has such a negative connotation for some people that the term keeps changing—to *resource development* or *advancement*, for example. It cracks me up, but I get it. I didn't like fundraising for a long time, even though I was good at the process and techniques. Once I figured out the Impact Triangle, I just focused on the relationships and my perspective, and it became the most rewarding thing I did. If you haven't experienced amazing results yet, it may be the psychology behind fundraising that is the obstacle. So let's dig into that.

Why do most volunteers want to run screaming into the hills when it's time to fundraise? They are uncomfortable with something, and it's important to determine what that is in order to move past it. For many it's a lack of confidence in knowing how to fundraise, or how to tell the organization's story. For others, it's not being clear about what is expected of them. Still others might fear rejection or some type of negative response. The first step is to help them realize that no one is going to die from fundraising. Then you need to step up like the leader you are, either as a volunteer peer or as staff, and help them get over it. Your mindset matters.

Remember, these are volunteers. They are (or should be, and will be) your primary fundraisers, and they *want* to be there with you. They can walk away if they wish…but they don't. Wow! Even though they might not be comfortable at first, what they aren't saying out loud is that they want to help, and they want to get comfortable and be successful. They want to learn. They did not get up today and say, "Let's see how badly I can screw up for the organization." You don't have a bunch of whiners on your hands; you have people who are a little anxious. This is good news, and I hope it inspires you. Now believe what is possible, and help develop volunteers who will embrace the notion of being philanthropic leaders.

These folks are sticking with you because of the relationship you and the team have formed. Yes, they believe in the mission for which you are all raising the money. But there are a lot of people who believe in your mission that aren't standing next to you during fundraising season. So what is it that keeps them volunteering for your organization? They like you and trust you, and they are generous. They feel a strong connection to the organization and value its impact on the community. They see this work as an honor, and as being bigger than themselves in a way that is rewarding.

At times it is easy to get caught up in the schedule and the numbers. But remember that these wonderful volunteers are taking time away from family or work to advance this cause. As your volunteer team creates your development plan, I would encourage you to incorporate intentional systems to acknowledge and support them regularly. Write it in as part of the group's expectations, and rotate responsibility and the type of activity. It can occur as a simple but genuine phone call to leadership, or a happy hour for the whole group.

The point is that this is an opportunity to deepen relationships and appreciate the village of folks surrounding you who are grateful to be a part of your important work. Focus on the goal, think about how it can be met, and make a choice to act.

CHAPTER TWENTY-ONE

RATE YOURSELF—THE AUDIT

I BELIEVE THAT IF YOU are feeling in a rut or confused about a situation, reassessing it is a productive way to jump-start your next move. Another reason to review the current state is to ascertain what strategies have been working well, where opportunities lie, and what pitfalls to avoid. This applies to all aspects of your organization. So conduct an audit of your current development efforts as a great first step toward your next initiative.

Some benefits of this internal assessment are:

- Identifying gaps and challenges needing attention
- Establishing a benchmark for future performance
- Creating priorities and longer-term strategic direction
- Understanding the importance of comprehensive planning and proven practices
- Engaging the team

Regarding the process, I recommend that board members and staff both participate. It doesn't have to be a grueling process; just be as honest and objective as possible. You will probably discover some areas in which you're doing a good job. And you may also uncover some areas needing attention, so be open to it. A well-informed board member from the development committee, another board member who is well respected, the executive director, and the development director, if there is one, are all good folks to have involved in the audit.

You should be able to complete the audit in one meeting if all the information is gathered in advance. The tricky part is making strong recommendations, which would be appropriate for the development committee to address, and then present them to the whole board. If you don't have a development committee, then the executive committee might be the next best choice to manage the process.

Where to Begin?

I am making an assumption that you have a written development plan. If you don't, then you can use this outline as a starting point for creating one, as well as the information in the next chapter. There are many examples of audit templates, and you can format your plan any way you wish. But there are key components to review, and I suggest you include these:

- **Alignment with strategic plan.** Determine whether your current plan is truly supporting the overall areas of focus of the organization. Why are you raising funds? Is the money being designated accordingly? Is the organization's need for funding clearly defined?
- **Who is involved?** Implementing the development plan is the work of many—it requires a team. It is *not* the responsibility of the development director alone; that person's role is to facilitate and coach, not actually fundraise. Surprised? The board must be heavily involved, as well as the executive director. Assessing this level of commitment from these leaders could be a key component as you plan for your next steps in creating philanthropic leadership.
- **The written case for support.** It is concise, yet tells the story of what urgent community needs are being met with funds raised by your organization. This may include some data, as well as testimonials from beneficiaries. It positions the organization as uniquely qualified to address critical needs. It shows donors where the money is being spent and how their investment is being utilized for good.

▶ **Human resources.** This can get a little sticky. The reality is that in order to deliver on a comprehensive plan, there needs to be some development staff. They can be volunteers, interns, or paid employees. The executive director alone cannot execute the plan well in addition to his or her other important duties. So the question becomes, are we adequately staffed to reach the goal? And are the people in place getting the support they need? In most cases, having a development director report to the executive director is the most effective structure. And a dedicated development committee that provides oversight to activities can be a very valuable resource; they direct the board's attention to areas needing support or acknowledgment.

▶ **Policies and procedures.** Is there a board giving policy (and I certainly hope it's expected that 100 percent of board members are making a stretch gift of which they are proud!)? What is the expectation for staff giving? Is there a gift acceptance policy? Can pledges be paid in installments throughout the year? How friendly is online giving?

▶ **Performance to metrics.** In reviewing the past three years of data, have the goals been reached? In what areas? Do you feel like you're measuring the right things? Donor retention, percentage of growth in gift amounts, how prospects are being qualified, and amount raised by the board are a few of the key performance indicators to monitor and evaluate. What trends are exciting or worrisome? It is vital to track the effectiveness of each solicitation strategy (event, direct mail, individual campaign, endowment, crowd funding, etc.).

▶ **Technology management.** Having the right donor database management system is critical, and there are several good systems to utilize. Can you easily generate reports showing top donors in certain categories over several years? Do you know your funding mix and what percentages account for which sources? Is it simple to see how individual donors are giving (events, annual appeal, online, planned giving, capital, etc.)? Can you tell who the campaigner/solicitor for each gift was? If you are frustrated with the information or lack of information you are getting from your system, call in support from the vendor. After some training, you may determine it's time to switch systems if you can't reach a satisfactory level of functionality. And if you are just starting, talk to colleagues about their experiences with different systems, too.

- **Diversity.** Do you feel there is enough diversity in your funding sources? Are you relying too heavily on government grants? (Thirty percent is generally considered the safe ceiling.) Does your annual campaign get much attention? How about planned giving, and direct mail? While you don't want to overextend yourself and your resources, it's good to look at your overall goals—short and long term—to best strategize annual activities.

- **Donor care.** Do you have a deliberate plan for identifying and cultivating prospects and engaging donors? How do you communicate with them? How often? Are recognition efforts impressive? Do you show them how you are being good stewards of their investments? The significance of these efforts cannot be overstated. Donors will give where they feel they can make an impact, where they are connected, and where they are treated with respect.

- **Education and support.** Both volunteers and staff need to know and understand the development plan. They need to understand why the strategies were chosen. They need to understand the psychology behind asking for money and how to articulate the case for support. They need to be trained on the logistics—what materials are to be used; what technology is available to assist; with whom, how, and when they communicate, and who can help if they get stuck. What is the timeline? It is a staff function to prepare and provide this information. Involving volunteers in delivery is great, but be clear—staff members are responsible for ensuring everyone on the team is ready to rock and roll.

- **Adhere to the AFP Code of Ethical Principles and Standards.** The Association of Fundraising Professionals has created standards that are commonly accepted and used by the industry. They outline appropriate practices for compensation, maintaining confidentiality, uses of funds, presentation, and much more. It is worthwhile to share this document with staff and volunteers.

Now while reading this, you may have broken into a sweat and felt a bit overwhelmed, especially if you were auditing your program in your head as you read. Take a breath and relax. Check your mindset. Even if everything isn't perfect in your development efforts, you now have a place to start. And you will take the next step with your trusted village of champions. You may be surprised what you accomplish as you move toward greater success. It will take time, but it is exciting to be a part of change and improved results. First you need to know where you are starting, and the audit will help you do that.

CHAPTER TWENTY-TWO

DEVELOPING THE COMPREHENSIVE PLAN

COMPREHENSIVE IS THE KEY word here. I wish I had a lift ticket for each time someone asked me for help with a specific development component, and when I asked how it fit into the overall development plan, the person wasn't sure. But that's okay, because we'll address all this here and you will be well equipped with a great plan.

Now that you have conducted an audit, you have a good sense of what has been working for your organization and in what areas you would like to stretch your thinking. Before we get into the steps of developing a great plan, I want to clarify the roles of the people involved.

▶ **Volunteers**. It is the board's role to lead the fundraising efforts by adopting a plan that is recommended by the development committee, executing key parts of it, and monitoring progress toward goals. (You will read my thoughts on the board's role in annual giving in the next two chapters.) Non-board volunteers will be involved in various fundraising functions also, such as committees, individual solicitations, events, and promotion. This is an excellent way to expand the number of storytellers out in the community.

Now, this may be a new concept to some board members. Perhaps they thought it was staff's job to fundraise. It's a true team effort. Can you be a champion for influencing change regarding this concept if needed? What will it take to manage some resistance? These are valid questions, and some strategies may need to be identified in advance of making the big announcement. I can see it now: "Guess what, everybody? We each get to go raise $10,000— yippee!" And the sound of silence is deafening. Remember to nurture your relationships and engage folks early in the conversation.

▶ **Staff.** Regardless of how your organization is structured, the development staff and/or executive director are responsible for recommending a plan for consideration, executing parts of it, and assisting in the monitoring of progress toward goals. Staff also provide materials, educate and train volunteers where appropriate, and otherwise support facilitation of the fundraising process. Notice that I have not said it is the staff's role to fundraise. While the executive director and some other key staff may be involved in submitting proposals or asking for major gifts, the responsibility falls on the shoulders of the board to ensure the organization is well resourced.

Now on to the steps in developing the plan that hopefully will be created by a committee comprised of board members, the executive director and/or development director, and perhaps other volunteers. The plan is based on the premise that the key steps in raising funds are identifying prospects, cultivating prospects, inviting them to invest, thanking donors, and stewardship.

(The following is excerpted and adapted from the *AFP First Course in Fundraising*.)

1. **Outline the purpose.** Ensuring that everyone understands the need for an annual development plan is the first step, so explain the general reasoning behind it. The plan will support the organization's operating goals for the current year, which in turn is one factor in advancing the strategic plan. An example of a need could be to underwrite the cost of expanding a program to new locations so the number of people served can double.

2. **Establish financial goals.** Each strategy will have an identified dollar goal. Use data from past years to determine how much you want to stretch.

I always encourage increasing goals over previous years unless there is an extenuating circumstance. You are not striving for mediocrity; you have people to serve, and you need all board members to take this seriously.

3. **Develop strategic goals (non-monetary).** These relate to the way you will achieve the plan. What will you focus on this year for best results? Examples could include new communication tactics, tightening up board solicitation, expanding prospect identification systems, implementing a new software system, or expanding donor cultivation practices. I recommend choosing no more than six to eight key strategies, or it becomes too much to manage.

4. **Confirm solicitation methods.** This is where you decide what will get you the best results. I want to point out here that a mix of methods is most effective. It's not unlike keeping a diversified investment portfolio. I have seen an organization that had traditionally been funded primarily by grants really struggle during the recession that hit hard in 2008. Government funding started to diminish, and there was no backup plan. So consider all options carefully. Options include individual annual giving, planned giving, special events, grants, direct mail, mobile and social media, crowd funding (Kickstarter and Indiegogo are two companies to check out; Causecast is a company that develops tools to help businesses engage with their employees by supporting the causes they care about), third-party events, major gifts, and capital. Each of these campaigns will then have listed a dollar goal, a timeline, specific strategies, and who is accountable.

NOTE: Once you have identified the fundraising activities that will work best for you, I hope you will include monthly giving as one of the strategies for individual campaigns. Not only will it likely raise more money for your mission work (if you ask someone for $100 once you get $100, but if you ask them for $25 a month you get $300) but it can help you retain donors longer. Also, inviting donors to make a multi-year commitment can be beneficial to both the community and the donor in terms of impact, but you must steward the relationship!

5. **Establish a communication plan.** This refers to efforts to promote the company's development activities and cultivate relationships with potential donors. Items to consider include the annual report, website, non-ask events, newsletters, and other public relations activities. Have a well-developed case for support that tells the story of your mission, and demonstrates impact, as a critical component for communication materials.

6. **Monitoring.** As mentioned before, it is the role of both staff and the board to follow and assess progress. Staff will provide data and the development committee will review and discuss issues as well as regularly report to the board. I can't stress enough how important it is to have development as a regular agenda item at board meetings. You cannot expect volunteers to be inspired and engaged if they are in the dark. At the end of each year, a formal evaluation should also occur, which will influence changes for improvement in the future.

7. **Calendar.** Once the plan is outlined, an annual calendar identifying what activities will be conducted by month is crucial to the process. As with anything, what gets written down gets done. This will drive the work of the development committee.

8. **Recognition.** When it comes to raising funds, take time to appreciate progress and effort. I encourage you to plan for it, and to work it into the annual timeline. It would be easy to chug away toward the next priority without even taking a breath. Well, let's make sure that recognizing your development team of staff and volunteers is high on the list of things to do. With development, there are tangible goals that are established: recruiting a certain number of volunteers, raising so many dollars, holding certain events, implementing a key cultivation strategy, updating the case, etc. So at each milestone, acknowledge the team who made it happen. Keep in mind what matters to them and celebrate accordingly. There are varying degrees of success, too. I don't mean to imply you should host a grandiose dinner every time a $500 gift is received. Sometimes a sincere phone call from the board president is most appropriate. The point is—think about it in advance, and incorporate recognition into your plan.

The Case for Support

It is very common for us to get tripped up here. As great as you may be at planning, and understanding effective strategies for raising funds, it's not unusual to be less confident about telling the incredible story of how your organization impacts the community. You may create several versions of your case to address different programs or services; you may also have the short and long version depending on who is using it and in what way. For example, a written grant proposal may require a lot of explanation, but when educating board members on how to tell the story, a one-page summary of key points is more effective.

There are some necessary components to writing a great case, and it can be fun to create. Let's take a look.

- It's critical that you understand why you need to raise money in the first place. What _critical community need or problem_ are you trying to address? Being able to state that right up front grabs attention. You can use a few statistics, but don't overdo it or your audience will lose interest. Think about painting a picture for them. An example could be, "Every night in our city at least 1,700 kids are sleeping under bridges, in cars, or on park benches."
- By providing some _history about the organization_, you build credibility. If you have been in business a long time, emphasize that. Speak to your mission and its focus on solutions to the need.
- Then show _what you do well_ in terms of meeting that need. Now you are speaking to purpose and impact. You are outlining the solution that needs support. An example could be, "Our organization provides three hundred meals and beds every day, and teaches life skills though our transitional living program."
- How do you stand out; _what makes you unique?_ If you are the only organization in the area tackling youth homelessness, say so. If you are run strictly by volunteers, let people know. If you incorporate academics into the program, shout it from the rooftops. You are special, and many potential donors may not know it and would love to invest in the solution.
- Share a specific, _true story_ about someone who benefited from your services. This testimonial could be the most important part of your case. It's emotional and

personal, and the details about an individual are meaningful. This hook may greatly influence the behavior of funders. (And by the way, it's a great time to reflect on why you do this work in the first place—mission at work!)

▶ Outline where the gaps are and why you need funding. _How will the money be used?_ What is the goal? For example, "This year we are raising $150,000 to offset the costs of meals, blankets, and jackets for two hundred children. Your investment of $500 will care for one child for six months, and is greatly appreciated."

▶ Then reiterate that together you can work to minimize the tragic effects of youth homelessness. Remember, this isn't about you or the organization; it's about the critical need in the community. _Bring the value back to them_ so they understand the power of their gift to the community.

We focused on planning in Part Two of this book. The great thing about planning is that once you do it the first time, it gets easier. In year two, you can look back and see where things went well and where you missed the mark. Then adjust and move forward. It's about focus. If you choose to simply latch on to every good idea that comes along, you will be scattered and it will show in the results. The community will pay the ultimate price.

So focus on the Impact Triangle—is your head in the game? Have you lined up your village of champions? Then grab your case and get moving!

CHAPTER TWENTY-THREE

EXECUTION WILL MAKE OR BREAK YOU

BACK IN CHAPTER 8 we talked about executing a strategic plan, and most of that content is also relevant to executing a development plan. But who is responsible for implementation?

I believe that development is one of the best places to form partnerships and teams. *No one person or committee is responsible for delivering success.* A savvy executive director and board president will strategically place board members in positions to succeed. Keep in mind that staff support the process. Managing up to the board is an important, and at times delicate, skill. It is essential to be crystal clear about expectations when the plan is introduced. And be prepared for questions, and even resistance, if the plan calls for new and untested strategies. So whether you are a member of the board, a program volunteer, or any level of staff, clarify your role and step up to help implement the plan.

For instance, board members are primarily responsible for the annual giving campaign. That means they are identifying prospects, and introducing those prospects to the organization. But they can't do any of this if staff haven't worked alongside them to make sure they are equipped. Conversely, I hope volunteers will understand that the additional work of a campaign falls onto already very full plates in terms of the staff's workload. As staff work to create documents, schedule meetings, and otherwise support the process, patience and recognition from the board is appreciated. There is an opportunity here to create a culture of team accountability.

Making It Come Alive

Now that the development committee has created a strong plan to effectively fund the organization, holding each other accountable for implementation is where the rubber meets the road. Funding the organization means you are advancing the mission and creating a noticeable social change. You cannot afford to miss the mark, or the community suffers.

Your plan will have a timeline with key benchmarks, and as outlined in the planning chapter, there are several ways to ensure the steps get executed:

- ▶ Use dashboards that highlight key metrics to stay on track.
- ▶ Communicate progress in committee and board meetings, as well as in electronic updates as appropriate to donors, members, and other key stakeholders.
- ▶ Ensure there are adequate resources to support development activities (people, money, facilities, technology, etc.).
- ▶ Adapt as needed when unexpected factors could affect outcomes.
- ▶ Evaluate progress toward goals annually for continuous improvement.
- ▶ Involve board members to influence peer behavior. This is a powerful strategy. Sometimes a volunteer agrees to work on a task or project, and then falls short for whatever reason. If another volunteer follows up to identify the obstacle and support the first person, odds are good that progress will be made. They respect each other's position and effort, and want to work together. When the executive director tries the same type of follow-up, it may still be effective, but the dynamic is different and the volunteer knows the director is just doing his or her job. It is a subtle difference, but a difference worth noting that can affect lasting impact.

The goal is to deliver on a plan that has been operationalized into the culture. The steps are repeatable because systems are in place to sustain the work.

So as the time approaches for the next development strategy, think of the Impact Triangle and check your mindset first. Are you open to the possibility of a rewarding team effort with the rest of your crew? Most people stay connected to an organization or job because of the relationships they form. So review the monitoring systems you incorporated into the development plan, and choose to embrace what's possible with your team.

CHAPTER TWENTY-FOUR

THE FIVE STEPS TO BOARD SUCCESS IN FUNDRAISING

AS WITH THE OTHER PROJECTS and initiatives you face, board fundraising can be highly successful when you apply the Impact Triangle principles. Ask yourself these questions:

- ▶ What is your mindset when you consider board fundraising?
- ▶ If you are an executive director, are you creating barriers that keep board members at arm's length?
- ▶ If you are a board member, are you hesitant to jump into unchartered waters?

Take an honest look at why there may be consistent issues around fundraising—the real underlying cause of the problem. Understanding this is critical to initiate change. If there is a tendency to think board members are too busy, don't want to commit, or will get too close to operations, then that will be your reality. So understand the issue, acknowledge it, and choose to resolve it.

Consider this:

- ► Are the right people in the right spots?
- ► Look around for your champions. Are the volunteers with whom you are well connected rising to the occasion?
- ► Are they leaders whom others will respond to when they are needed?
- ► Are the board members well connected in the community so expectations can be met?
- ► Do staff members have the right skill set to facilitate development? Are there enough of them?
- ► This is a key place to leverage your relationship capital so you can fund your mission.
- ► What has been done to truly develop volunteers?

Both board members and staff have a responsibility here. The tools and resources for successful orientations, creating fundraising plans, and engaging volunteers have been around for years. Building a strong team of board members takes work and dedication, and there is no way around it. When you have the right players in place, they will want to perform well and will want you to guide them toward success.

As you know, fundraising is a team effort. Each organization is different, and executive directors and board presidents will come up with different places to start. Don't get hung up on what the exact right next step is; just start talking to the players and asking good questions, and the answers will come.

I have seen many organizations simply get stuck, paralyzed in their resource development progress because the board isn't actively participating. It's a little scary how often this happens…but it doesn't need to be this way. Now, I'm a realist, and very few people will come skipping in your doors begging to be allowed to fundraise. But if you're recruiting well, board members very much want to support the mission. I am a strong proponent of "giving and getting." Let's make it less intimidating and easier for volunteers to do.

Some steps you can take:

- ► Examine what you truly believe about the board's performance in fundraising, and be willing to consider that it's time to look at things differently. If you're sincere, possibilities start to become clear. Change your mind, and change your results.

▶ Review your strategic goals around resource development that advance the mission. Outline specific tasks for teams/committees, then describe the role of individuals on those teams.

▶ Find examples of where fundraising is working and share those successes with board members and staff so they know it's possible to adjust and achieve goals.

▶ The key to all board performance is deep and consistent engagement. If there isn't an engagement and retention strategy for your organization, it's time to create one.

You Expect Me to *What*??

I don't know about you, but I'm not willing to accept that fundraising continues to receive the lowest rating across the United States regarding board performance. Not everyone can make the personal ask for a major gift, but everyone can participate in some way to develop resources for the organization.

Here are the steps to take to develop successful fundraising board members:

1. **Tell them you expect them to fundraise right at the start.** The first time you interview them about their board candidacy, tell them they are expected to personally invest, as well as to invite others to donate. If they are fighting the urge to go screaming into the hills, assure them that staff will provide them with all the tools they need to be successful, and create an individual strategy for them. If they do eventually join the board, review expectations in the board orientation. Ask for questions. Reassure them, have an experienced board member show how it has worked in the past, and start talking about the importance of identification and cultivation. Right here I just listed four ways to outline and support fundraising expectations—when you do this, there will be no surprises.

2. **Deal with the scary stuff early.** Remember the scary F word? This is all so normal! So talk about it and help volunteers understand that fundraising isn't about chasing down rich people. It's about having a strong mission and leveraging relationships in a way that matches the donor's

interests with community needs. When done well, potential donors will clearly see the opportunity to invest in solving a problem. Then they can make an educated decision about giving.

3. **Make good on the education promise—train them.** This is a staff responsibility, with support from members where appropriate. Schedule a separate coaching session and walk board members through a specific case for support (an even better strategy is to have volunteers create the case with staff; then everyone buys in, and they implement). Now they can comfortably articulate how the money will be utilized and what community needs will be met. This is a great time to have seasoned boards member tell their story about why they will be raising funds, which can serve to inspire rookies, or reiterate the importance of pulling together around this cause. Let them get some practice by role-playing with a specific prospect in mind. Provide the steps, materials, and resources they will need to be successful. A strong development program has many pieces, so focusing on the priorities is key here.

4. **Meet them where they are—individualize their role in the plan.** Try to match members' experience, personality, and skills to their fundraising activities. Not everyone will be ready to ask for a $5,000 gift. Here are examples of appropriate ways to get volunteers started:

   ► Start smaller, and learn how to ask current donors to increase the size of their gift.
   ► Some members will enjoy hosting a non-ask event at their home, which is a great cultivation activity.
   ► Others may want to start by posting a link to the donation page on their website or Facebook page.
   ► Perhaps a volunteer can introduce a grant writer who would like to do pro bono work.
   ► Every board member will be expected to review his or her connections and identify potential donors.

Note that there are many ways to get volunteers started…all with the end goal in mind—inviting others to make a gift. And keep in mind that it's much easier to ask someone else to invest after you have done so your-self. So creating a board solicitation strategy to kick-start the campaign is a wildly successful strategy. (See more below.)

5. **Support, listen and continue to develop board members.** Whether you are staff or a volunteer, fundraising is a team effort (I've said this before, haven't I?). It can be so rewarding, but at times also draining. Rely on your partnership to notice if some people are becoming burnt out. Who has been silent or missing lately? How can they best be supported? Sometimes just knowing others are standing beside them is enough to motivate board members to do the next thing. And while fundraising is an important part of any organization's work, it certainly isn't all you do. So be intentional about taking a break, celebrating, and looking at the big picture.

Board Solicitation Program

There are several reasons to take very seriously this step in your development efforts. If you just look at the practical side of things, many grant funders will not consider applicants who cannot say they have 100 percent board giving. Additionally, assuming you have a board giving policy that indicates all members of the board are expected to contribute, when you don't adhere to it the organization looks weak, and you can't expect others to get excited about investing.

Let's look at the psychology behind this for board members. How can they embrace the thought of asking others to get behind a cause financially if they haven't given in a way that makes them proud? I picture an actual scenario when I was with a well-connected board member on a call to ask a woman in his professional network for a $10,000 gift. We had strategized and agreed on who would take what role, and felt good about understanding what the prospective donor was most interested in and how we would match her interests to our mission. We got to her office, things were rolling along, and he choked. He was supposed to extend the invitation to give, and I realized he simply wasn't going to be able to come through. After a split second of panic (because I knew we might not get a second chance), I asked the woman to support the organization in tackling the community need with a gift of $10,000. She said she would be proud to do so, and asked what she needed to sign—*yes!*

As we were walking to the car, I asked my partner how he thought it went. He said, "I'm so glad you were there. I just couldn't get myself to ask her." After some probing questions, he admitted that he hadn't made his commitment yet. He was hanging his head and dragging his feet the way my son did when he was three years old and had to tell me he'd tipped over a plant and spilled dirt all over our light carpet. I realized I had an opportunity in front of me. So I simply asked him if making a pledge to contribute $5,000 (I knew his giving history, of course) would clear that feeling up for him. He smiled and said, "Absolutely. Thanks for asking me to commit."

It was a unique and strange interaction for me. And then I clearly understood what my CEO had told me once—that our board members, who are the innermost circle of our work, deserve the respect of a personal invitation to give. From that point forward, I ferociously approached the board giving process with deliberation. I hope you will consider including a version of this system into your development plan.

Sending out an email reminding your members about the commitment they made when they joined the board isn't enough. Expecting them to enthusiastically reply with a generous gift promise isn't realistic. Do you want to engage your volunteers and help them feel appreciated? Then keep reading and learn how to create a meaningful board giving policy.

Have a clear written expectation that addresses board members giving and getting. Here's the deal. All board members must financially invest, as we know. They must also participate in fundraising (that dirty word). As we've discussed, there are different ways to do so that utilize their individual strengths and leverage resources.

But be specific—how much do you want them to give? How much do they need to raise? Notice I used the word *individual* above. My strong belief is that these expectations will vary from member to member. It takes a little more work to think through and ends up leading to greater results—not just financially, but also in terms of engagement.

How do you communicate these expectations? One way to accommodate for various levels of capacity in terms of giving is to state a category of giving. So if you have a Founders Club that includes gifts between $5,000 and $10,000, use that designation and list it on your expectations sheet, "Board members are expected to contribute financially at least at the Founders Club level." That range provides flexibility and clearly says that if you are not able to donate at least $5,000, this board may not be right for you. Also, be prepared to answer questions about what the average board gift is at present.

A strong board solicitation strategy isn't just about clarifying expectations, however. Beyond that, you want to influence how individual members feel about their participation. This can be an engagement strategy that carries a long-lasting and deep value for board members. It positions them to be more genuinely passionate about their effort to develop resources for the organization, and ultimately the community.

Put together a small team of board members with the executive director who serve as strong champions of board giving. There may only need to be one organizational meeting each year to reach a consensus on strategy. The idea is to assign each board member to a member of this team, who will ask them for their annual gift. The commitment to meet with each volunteer personally is significant, so be sure to recruit this team well. Once the board assignments are made, then individual strategies can be discussed.

Be aware of the sensitive issues around confidentiality here. For veteran board members who have been giving regularly, the strategy may be to ask each to increase his or her gift by 20 percent. For new board members, it will be important to estimate capacity and refer to a range of giving. Here is one thing I've learned: the majority of people will not be offended if you ask for an amount higher than they are able to reach. There is something that resonates when you flatter them by thinking they are capable of a larger gift.

Your team should be educated on the power of asking for a specific amount or range. And none of the board members will be surprised, since this was covered in the recruitment process, again at the orientation, and again when the development plan was approved by the board. Right? Regardless of the strategy and outcome, only the executive director and president of the board are entitled to know the gift amounts of any donor.

Make the ability to contribute easy and seamless. Most people can give more over time. So be sure to allow, and speak to your willingness to welcome, a commitment that can be paid in installments for their convenience. Again, monthly giving could sound much more palatable to some people. In addition, this should be a stretch gift of which they can be proud. That type of commitment is meaningful to the organization and the donors, and it enables them to feel confident when inviting their colleagues to join them in strengthening the community through the good work of your organization. I am assuming you have the ability to accept online donations, which is becoming a more preferable choice for many donors.

Then establish a timeline for completion of the meetings. If you have a small board, thirty days may be enough; a longer time period may be necessary for a large board. Whatever calendar you set up, the executive director should work hard to keep members of the team accountable. Send out weekly progress reports to motivate (being careful not to list individual pledges, just totals—this is confidential!).

If a systematic approach to board solicitation sounds complicated or burdensome to you, I will argue the opposite. It has made a sustainable and significant difference for many organizations. From personal experience, I have seen very positive results. In addition to creating an opportunity for individual volunteers to feel valued and inspired, it sets the stage for successful development. Leveraging the generosity of the board to launch an annual giving campaign is powerful! Imagine being able to say that 40 percent of the goal has been achieved right up front because of the commitments from the board. That will send a strong message to the community, as well as inspire board members to be champions for your cause.

CHAPTER TWENTY-FIVE

THE ANATOMY OF THE INVITATION

NOW THAT EVERYONE IS on board with the development strategy and eager to get started, let's make sure they know how to extend an invitation to invest in the community. First we need to think about vocabulary.

Most fundraisers have been trained to prepare for the "ask." I am not in love with that word. In fact, I look at it differently. I believe that if we are doing our jobs well, we have to earn the right to approach someone. This shift can be significant in shaping your mindset. Additionally, I like to think of a donation as a "gift" and donating as "giving," or better yet, "investing." Donors (investors) trust you to leverage their dollars into some type of change in the community—that is an investment.

When you are sincere and purposeful, you no longer feel like you are chasing money, or feel guilty about taking money, but instead you are developing another person's interest in the mission. In doing so, you have nurtured and cultivated the relationship with the prospective donor, and as a stakeholder of the organization, you have an obligation to "invite" that person to get involved.

There are five basic steps to individual, relationship-based fundraising:

I. Identification
Most board members who are new to development feel as though they don't know

anyone to ask. This is often a result of thinking that only rich people donate, and most of us don't know a lot of rich people. Keep in mind:

- Seven out of 10 households make charitable contributions.
- The top reason people donate is because they have a connection to the organization. They know you, or someone who has benefitted from your services, or perhaps they attended an event or volunteered.
- They also believe in your mission and think the work of the organization is good for the community.

So when you educate your board members about who gives, and why people give, it becomes easier to identify potential donors.

The process can be simplified for your board members by having them make a list of the people they know at work, neighbors, colleagues, social media friends and connections, family members, personal friends, people from their alumni groups, service club members, parents of their kids' friends, people who have asked them to support their charities, vendors, book club and poker club members, clients, and others.

From there, ask them to prioritize the list by those who are likely to be most interested in the mission of the organization. You will gain better results if you do this activity with each individual rather than in a group, but typically most volunteers can identify several people whom they feel would be interested in learning more about the organization.

II. Cultivation

Here's a good story from several years ago. A colleague of mine came into my office and slumped down in a chair. With lower lip protruding and eyes downcast, she proceeded to tell me she just got turned down when asking a potential donor for $25,000. I empathized, because that experience can take the wind out of your sails. She elaborated, and I realized she may have skipped a step in the relationship. As a matter of fact, when I asked her how long she had known this person, she said, "I met him once about three weeks ago and he seemed really nice." *Uh-oh.*

As it turned out, he barely knew her and she certainly had not earned the right to invite him to invest at that level. Hard lesson. The point is you that must get to know potential donors. Cultivation is usually *the longest part of the process*. Once you know what a person is interested in, have developed a trusting relationship, and moved the person closer to the organization, then you can consider extending an invitation.

Cindi's Top Ten Cultivation Techniques to Build Relationships:

10. Provide a tour of the facility.
9. Send personal messages with the newsletter or other mass communications from the organization.
8. Invite people to meet the board president, executive director, and/or beneficiaries of the organization's programs and services.
7. Send them holiday, birthday, and congratulatory notes.
6. Invite them to your special event.
5. Send them articles about their areas of interests (skiing, theater, college, concerts, etc).
4. Invite them to a non-ask event, hosted by a board member, to learn more about the organization and meet volunteers and guests.
3. Ask them to speak on, or write an article about, their areas of expertise for your board, staff, or beneficiaries.
2. Include an interesting story about them in your newsletter.
1. Ask for advice—in person—on topics that are important to your organization (for example, future plans or key projects).

However you choose to interact with a prospective donor, it needs to be relevant and feel natural to both of you. If it's forced or disingenuous, the person will see right through it and doubt your integrity. You don't want it to backfire, so be thoughtful in your approach. Remember, the goal is to earn the right to invite this person to invest in the community.

III. Invite to Invest

At some point, you will feel as though you can take the next step. There is no formula to tell you when, so just trust your gut. For major gifts or lead capital gifts, it could take much longer than for smaller gifts. Whenever the time comes, keep these tips in mind:

- Tell your story. Tell your prospective donors why you are involved in the organization. What compelled you to work or volunteer here?
- Share the case for support that will outline the urgent need they connect to emotionally. Provide some history and explain how the organization is uniqely positioned to provide solutions.
- Provide the testimonial of a person who benefitted from the programs and services.
- Then invite the person to join you in investing in the community. *Note:* It's not about the organization's needs; your organization is just a pass-through vehicle. The funds will be used to strengthen the community.
- Connect a specific-size gift to a tangible need. An example might be, "I hope you will invest $1,000 that will provide mentoring services to fifty boys this year." Your donors will feel good about the value of their investment.
- Thank them!
- **Power Tip**: Ask donors who else they know who might be interested in learning more about the organization! You want to expand your donor base and increase awareness of your great work, right? Who better to help achieve that goal than your investors?

Okay, I know. You want to know what to do when someone says no. And people will. Relax. What is the worst thing that is going to happen? It's not as bad as you think.

First of all, there are four kinds of no:

1. No, not now or ever
2. No to the timing
3. No to the amount
4. No to the project

You may be able to overcome the last three, in which case it's appropriate to continue the conversation. In fact, I would argue that you have an obligation to the community to continue the conversation. Maybe then, maybe later. But ask what is keeping people from investing, and see if you can overcome the obstacle.

Maybe they just don't care about what you are trying to fund. Ask them what might interest them more.

Maybe they can't commit this month. Ask them to make a pledge and then pay on it at their convenience, and offer installment options.

Maybe they can't invest at that level. Every single gift is needed and appreciated, so help them feel good about any amount they can give. At some other time, they may feel more comfortable at a higher level.

Finally, remember that you just shared an important story about the organization. You increased awareness and perhaps have a new advocate for your mission. Getting a no is far from a failure.

IV. Thank and Recognize

No matter the result of the conversation, always show your gratitude. Thank people for their time, their gift, and/or their willingness to identify others who might want to get involved. In addition to what you do already, such as sending a thank-you letter with tax information provided, I hope you will brainstorm ideas with your development committee on a recognition system. Some people prefer to give anonymously, but most donors are proud of their support and don't mind the acknowledgment.

I would encourage you to think about how your recognition efforts can be unique. A plaque on the wall or a token gift for the desk is nice. And boring. More donors these days are requesting that none of their fundraising dollars be used for recognition, so the money can all go to direct service. So get creative and have fun with it! There are plenty of resources online to get you started.

V. Involve and Steward

I saved the most critical step for last. You want to retain your donors. How will you do that? Do not leave it to chance or you will find yourself spending most of your time looking for new donors. You started to get your donors closer to the organization during the cultivation stage. You did such a great job that they invested. Now you must continue to build the relationship and show them how you are investing their gifts.

It goes beyond just thanking them. Show them the difference you are making by sharing an impact report. It doesn't have to be complicated—I like infographics that are simple and have visuals showing data, as well as a photo or two. Include a note from or about a beneficiary of services, if practical.

The organization charity: water does a wonderful job of this. They strive to bring clean drinking water to developing countries and they take great pride in showing how the money raised is used. They provide photos, stories and actual GPS coordinates of where individual projects have been completed. For a wonderful example of reporting back to donors, check them out at www.charitywater.org

And continue your cultivation efforts. Only about 20 percent of your donors may truly want to get further involved, but don't be shy about inviting them to serve on a committee, or perhaps eventually the board. Maybe they would be interested in volunteering for an open house or as a mentor. What if they helped you raise money and served as an advocate in the community? Maybe they have a family member who wants to work with an organization with a social mission.

There are many ways to continue the relationship that serves both the donor and the organization. Again, be intentional and focus on the relationships and priorities that will move your mission forward. And always, always remember the Impact Triangle.

Summary of Key Points

1. Earned revenue is an important part of the formula for sustainability. Having a diverse revenue stream is good business practice, and organizations that assess and innovate will position themselves well for future success.

2. The psychology around fundraising is real, so the need to address it and equip the team to feel confident and capable is real, too.

3. Conducting a development audit will identify strengths, opportunities, gaps, and priorities as well as engage the team and establish benchmarks.

4. An audit looks at how efforts are aligned with the strategic plan: are all the right people involved, is there a strong case, are appropriate policies in place, is there performance toward goals, are there diverse revenue streams, is the right technology in place, are donors being engaged and volunteers being trained, and are ethical practices in place?

5. It takes a strong team to fundraise well and it is the board's role to lead the effort in a variety of ways, with staff playing a supporting role.

6. The steps in creating a development plan are outlining the purpose, determining financial goals, creating strategic goals, confirming solicitation methods, developing the communication plan, establishing a monitoring system, attaching a timeline to it, and outlining recognition strategies.

7. The case for support is an integral part of the foundation for fundraising—it must create a sense of urgency and inspire passion for the mission, resulting in the desire to invest.

8. Execution of the development plan is dependent upon a culture of team accountability. Use the monitoring systems identified.

9. Many will say it's very hard, if not impossible, to successfully involve the board in fundraising. Not true! Mindset is critical. Align volunteer interests or skills with appropriate tasks, and stay committed to the engagement process.

10. The five steps to creating fundraising volunteers are to be clear about expectations when recruiting; speak in terms of mission and leveraging relationship capital (not chasing money) to reduce anxiety; train them on how to invite others to support the community; realize each member

will participate in different ways; and focus on their strengths, listen, and support them throughout the program.

11. Inviting someone to invest in your organization includes identification of prospects, cultivation, inviting, thanking, and stewardship.

12. Be sure to have a written board giving policy and launch a deliberate, peer-to-peer board solicitation process.

Action Steps

1. Task the finance committee with evaluating the diversity of revenue sources. If needed, consider including this topic on a board meeting agenda to inspire volunteers to brainstorm some strategies to diversify.

2. Conduct an objective development audit, to include an analysis of board member attitudes toward fundraising.

3. Using the audit results, refine your current plan, or put together a team to create your first development plan.

4. Working with the governance committee and development committee, review the board giving policy as well as board expectations for fundraising. Are they clear? Have you set up the board for success? Are you holding everyone accountable for resourcing the organization?

5. Conduct a board education session focused on individual giving and the art of extending an invitation to invest in the community.

6. Spend time refining your donor relationship program. Do you need to focus on some stewardship activities?

PART FIVE

APPLYING THE IMPACT TRIANGLE TO BUILDING THE POTENTIAL IN STAFF

5

CHAPTER TWENTY-SIX

WHAT'S THE POINT?

"The growth and development of people is the highest calling of leadership."
—Harvey Firestone

I LOVE THIS QUOTE. I truly believe that knowing how to help others be their best is one of the most valuable skills a leader or supervisor can possess. Why? Running an important business means you need your A team around you. Being average does not get amazing results.

In a company with a social mission, you can't be less than amazing because too many others are counting on you. You are not selling widgets, you are impacting lives, and in some cases actually saving them. So do you want a team with a lackadaisical attitude? Do you want average performers? As you strive to meet the double bottom line, do you want mediocrity? I don't think you do, so don't settle for it.

Here are some of the benefits of leadership development:

- ▶ In addition to impact on the community, your team will feel valued when you commit to guiding their development. They will achieve a higher level of satisfaction.
- ▶ Communication, trust, and pride typically increase because of the spirit of collaboration.

▶ Professional development results in a higher level of staff retention. So in the end, you can spend less time recruiting volunteers and staff, and more time moving toward excellence.

▶ You are also developing bench strength. This builds the team, and it enables you to call on reserves if someone is out or moves on one day. Strengthening the collective wisdom of all players can significantly influence how, and at what pace, you achieve success.

▶ In the meantime, you can delegate more to these very talented team members. They will gain confidence and feel empowered to thrive in their roles.

▶ They will also be able to help train and lead others who come on board.

▶ When folks are feeling good about their experience, they tell others. So along with all these other benefits, your organization will gain a reputation for investing in their people and for being a great place to be involved. When it's a privilege and honor to be part of the company, you will attract more talent.

Investing energy in the right places that will increase your return on that investment is working smart.

The complaint I hear most often from supervisors is about how much time it takes to deal with personnel issues. And I will admit that yes, it does take time. The choice is whether the time is spent up front and continues in a supporting way or it is spent managing problems and troubleshooting issues because you didn't invest time earlier.

People are going to make mistakes that will require you to get involved in some way. But are they mistakes made while trying to learn and grow, while thinking outside the box and trying something new? Or are they making mistakes because they weren't trained, supported, or coached along the way?

Next we will focus on the development of people and the management of their performance. To be victorious at this, you must embrace the Impact Triangle— shift to the right mindset, understand the importance of relationships, and utilize the tools available.

CHAPTER TWENTY-SEVEN

PROFESSIONAL DEVELOPMENT HOW-TO'S

AS I WAS DOING RESEARCH for this book, I was intrigued by how the topic of development came up in unexpected places and surprising ways. Some executive directors dismissed staff development as a secondary need because they believed they hired well and assumed employees would learn and produce on their own. Others were desperate to understand how to achieve effective development plans when resources were tight. And then there were those who really didn't acknowledge, nor did they invest in, their staff because they were so focused on outcomes. I guess the thing that made all of this so intriguing to me is that it all resonates. I have felt all three of these things at some point in my career.

Let's define professional development first so you can wrap your head around it. I'll use this definition from www.freedictionary.com : "A process that assists individuals in an agency or organization in attaining new skills and knowledge, gaining increasing levels of competence, and growing professionally." So it is a process that takes time; it's not a training class. Professional development is learning, and it results in a more competent person. Sounds good to me. So now what?

The most successful organizations have leaders who understand the value of helping employees achieve their potential. I will always remember the time when I was doing a reference check and a former employer told me the candidate was excellent at bringing out the best in people. I was fortunate enough to have a strong pool of applicants, and this was the point that determined to whom I would extend an offer. I jumped at the chance to hire a person devoted to developing others, and it was true—she was an expert at inspiring others and helping them reach their potential. It was a great match for our team.

A note of clarification: When I use the word *staff*, this includes both paid and unpaid employees. So I am assuming you are treating and investing in your staff whether they are paid employees or volunteers. (This does not include board members who are policy volunteers.) You may want to do a quick check-in to see if you can validate this assumption. If not, why would you treat volunteers differently, or expect anything different from them, if they are helping you deliver on the mission?

The Goal Is to Create a Culture of Lifelong Learning

Regardless of your position in an organization, you have a responsibility to see that the business is successful, growing, and innovative. You don't accomplish this alone, and so the caliber of people around you is critical. The more capable the people, the more successful the organization will become. Thus it bears repeating that investing in professional development benefits everyone—the individual, the company, and the community being served by the social enterprise. Commit to internal greatness and position yourself for improved results.

When looking at this from the Impact Triangle perspective, our beliefs about development are important to examine:

- How have you invested in people?
- How effective have your efforts been?
- What do staff members think about those efforts, and how would they rate development strategies?
- Have you seen a change in performance as a result?
- Do you put off development activity because it costs too much or takes a lot of time?
- Is your team good enough already? Maybe they don't want to change anything.

Take a minute and think about it.

Whatever you discover here will affect your next move regarding staff development. I am hoping you see a parallel between investment and what is possible. I have yet to discover anyone who has not embraced the opportunity to learn, in one way or another. Not anyone. There has always been something a person wanted to know more about or improve. Your people are not striving to fail. They are hoping to do a great job—so help them be their best. You owe it to the community.

Who Does What?

Employees are responsible for their own learning. If they are to move up the career ladder, they must complete the necessary steps. If a person wants be the best staff director or program volunteer, he or she is responsible for doing what it takes.

Supervisors and leaders help create opportunity. How many times have you heard people say that they are stuck in a dead-end job, or their supervisor never teaches them anything new or sends them for training? It would be interesting to ask what they have done lately to ask for support and direction in this area. It takes a team to implement a good leadership development plan. When you hear these complaints, it's possible neither person truly understands his or her role.

There's one thing to be keenly aware of when it comes to professional development: one size does not fit all. The leader should outline some key strategies for development but recognize that individuals learn differently, and are motivated by different things. For example, one employee may really enjoy relationships with co-workers and participants and be motivated by social situations. Another could be motivated by achievement and need to understand very early on what metrics will be used to measure success. So working together to determine the most effective plan will be key to a successful effort.

We discussed engagement of board members in chapter 15. I would encourage you to refer to it again as you think about how to best involve your employees and volunteers in their own development. Interacting about something as personal as one's growth and learning has great potential for deepening relationships, and that alone can be motivating. And as you follow up and encourage and coach, you will likely see a more engaged team.

Knowing What You Need

The steps in professional development are not unlike the steps in most plans. First, you must identify what is needed to reach success. In a learning environment, we look at competencies. What skills, knowledge, attributes, or experience must a person have to be the most successful in the position? Outlining core competencies can be rather fun!

By starting with a clean slate, you can create an activity that engages staff to help identify these things. If you can encourage their ownership in the process, you are definitely off to a great start. I recognize that this isn't going to happen every time you bring on a new person, but there is something to be said for being able to point to the competencies that the team agreed are top priority.

If we use the example of a program director, which is a fairly common position in a nonprofit organization, there may be eight to twelve key competencies necessary for one to be successful. They could include communication, fiscal management, program development, leading others, decision making, inclusion, and working with volunteers. You can refer to job descriptions to get the brainstorming started, and then have members of the team vote on the most critical skills. I like the idea of having people who are not employed in that position being invited so they can weigh in too. They may be able to see things that you are blind to, and this outside perspective could prove valuable.

Once the key competencies are identified, it's time for some assessing. The employee will perform a self-assessment, and you will also assess the person in the desired areas. *Note:* Sometimes people get all freaked out when the word *assess* or *evaluate* is used because it can seem so personal. Well, then, depersonalize it and help shift that perspective. Make the conversation about performance and behavior, not about personality. This isn't a popularity contest. And remember that people want to learn and grow. Present this assessment as an opportunity. As time goes on and the culture really does become about learning, most of the sensitivity will dissolve. Understanding that this dynamic may exist in the relationship is important, and will help you carefully set a positive tone.

There may be some areas employees have very little experience in yet. All of us have areas to develop. I encourage you to frame the conversation in a way that clearly shows how this activity is designed to benefit them in their professional development, and what it will mean to the team, organization, and community when they excel. These folks are involved because they believe in the mission, so tie the competencies to the mission and help them see the connection. By being their best, they help deliver the impact of the mission. And showing your investment in their growth is a tangible way to show your support.

Continuing with the program director example, perhaps an employee is new to the budgeting process and does not feel confident. By choosing financial management as an area to develop, this person will feel supported and probably relieved. Now you both need to commit—you commit to finding opportunities for learning, and the employee commits to following through with these activities. Chances are good that your relationship will also deepen and the employee will feel more valued.

You can see how the Impact Triangle is in play here. We talked about mindset and some reflection questions. In addition, the relationships with your staff are essential in this process. Have you heard the saying, "Feed your staff so they don't eat you?" Once the development framework has been established, you can implement winning practices and the result will be very rewarding.

CHAPTER TWENTY-EIGHT

PROVIDING LEARNING OPPORTUNITIES

YOU MAY HAVE HEARD of the 70-20-10 Learning model based on research by Michael M. Lombardo and Robert W. Eichinger. The concept begins with the realization of a development need and the motivation to do something about it, and that a blend of different learning approaches can provide powerful learning.

The premise is that only 10 percent of adult learning comes from formal training. Workshops, webinars, college classes, research, and the like account for this type of learning. Does that surprise you? Many people think of professional development as being the next set of workshops they are going to attend. This model would indicate differently. And then 20 percent of learning is attributed to coaching, which includes feedback from various people and observing others.

The bulk of our learning comes from on-the-job experiences—about 70 percent. These opportunities need to be challenging in order for learning to occur, and many times they involve problem-solving. My experience would support the notion that reality teaches us the most. Knowing this, how can you best develop someone?

Let's focus on the 10 percent first. Formal trainings are usually the first type to pop to mind, and the easiest to plan.

- There may be conferences offered with relevant topics for learning.
- Your professional association may conduct webinars.
- The local support organizations for nonprofits may have trainings in areas ranging from computer literacy to fundraising management.
- The local community colleges are valuable resources also, and many universities have certificate programs now designed for working people.
- You also can hold workshops yourself, or ask a board member to come teach on his or her area of expertise if it will help advance professional development.

While it's fairly easy to identify and plan for these events, the caveat that causes us to hesitate is that they typically cost money. This is where you need to adopt a philosophy that will guide your decisions. Will professional development be one of the first things you cut when the budget gets tight? Will you commit to protecting at least some training resources? This isn't an easy question, and I would encourage you to think about it seriously.

You know what is best for your organization. The answer may partly depend on how "green" or advanced your team is now. If most staff members are deep into their development plans, it might be possible to delay some formal education for a bit. Even though only 10 percent of learning is attributed to formal trainings, I would caution you to not eliminate it from the budget. Your employees deserve the opportunity, and so does the community you serve.

Keep in mind your wonderful relationships. It is possible a friend, a board member, or a foundation would underwrite the cost of professional development if they see how it will benefit the organization in the long term. Can you demonstrate how an investment in professional growth will impact the community? This type of capacity building is gaining more attention by funders these days, so keep the option in your toolkit. I have seen it work well when results are measured and are sustainable going forward.

Now let's think about the coaching part of learning—the 20 percent. Coaching can be described as the ability to support a person's learning toward a shared goal, when it is mutually desired and individualized. (Note the word *mutually*—you cannot coach someone who does not want to be coached.) Coaching is a learned skill and is highly effective when done well, so give it a try.

The coach isn't providing the answers but is guiding, asking questions, and providing feedback so the employee can find a solution. You are guiding people as they develop a skill. Using the example of the program director who is motivated to improve her budgeting skills, think about who could guide that learning.

- Is there an experienced and trustworthy peer who could give tips? Does he or she have a strong relationship with the employee?
- Are you available to assist?
- The employee can also shadow a more experienced person, observe that person, and start doing basic tasks until ready to be left on his or her own.
- Role-playing is also an effective way to learn in a safe environment. This is about practicing and receiving feedback until learning has occurred.

A coach will observe employees' performance as they work through their trials and hold them accountable to their commitments. There may be some false starts, but knowing there is a partner who will support their learning is motivating to employees and builds confidence.

I have identified four steps in the coaching process: **DIAL.**

D At the beginning, you will want to **discover** what the issue is from the employee's perspective. What is the person trying to accomplish? What has been tried already? What are some of the obstacles? Who has been involved to date? This is where you gain some understanding and agree on the purpose of working together.

I Then the discussions can revolve around **identifying** possible solutions. You can ask the employee questions: *What would need to change in order to reach the desired goal? What other resources might be needed? What other research can be done to zero in on an answer? What is the top priority? What best aligns with our mission?* Sometimes it takes a few conversations to nail this down, but the goal is to identify one or two actionable options.

A It is time to **act** by putting a vetted solution to the test. You have discussed pros and cons. You will send people on their way, but be sure to schedule check-ins so you can support and monitor their progress. You can ask questions: *What worked well? What would you do differently? What have you learned?* And of course it's good to celebrate any step forward. Not every solution will be the best one; the first one may not work at all. But acknowledge the commitment to reach for success, and help people understand that it's a process. This could go a long way toward building their confidence.

L   Once it seems that an effective solution has been reached, review what has been **learned** in the process. Find out how people feel about their progress. To what extent is the solution sustainable? What will they apply to other situations going forward? How do they feel about the coaching process? By this time, employees will likely feel good about their development, and it is your job to congratulate them on being willing to be coached and point out any observations you had. Your feedback is valuable and can motivate them to continue to lean into challenges in the future.

On to the opportunities that comprise the bulk of our learning. This 70 percent is the real-life experiences that provide challenges and encourage us to move out of our comfort zone. I think it's important to pause here to talk about risk. This experiential learning model doesn't necessarily mean baptism by fire. Sometimes that will work in a low-risk situation such as putting together meeting packets. However, you would not tell the program director to just go ahead and develop the annual budget and hope the person figures it out along the way. The director would need training or coaching on history and trends, factors that influence projections, revenue mix, acceptable ratios, and other areas. Try to be intentional about how you are developing staff and volunteers.

Some examples of experiential opportunities for learning include:

► Inviting people to serve on a committee or work group for a new project in their area of interest; they will also learn about how to work as a team member.
► Fundraising—while they will certainly receive training, you can't do it for them. They will head out and ask for money on their own at some point.

- Sharing a book on presentation styles and having an employee lead the next orientation meeting.
- Having a person who is trying to hone his or her communication skills write an article for the newsletter.
- Encouraging people to join a networking group if they are striving to develop relationship-building skills.
- Asking them to research best practices in recruiting volunteers, and sharing findings with others.

In each of these examples, the goal is that people will learn and grow more confident through the experience, and with the right level of support. We can't always predict how situations will present themselves, so chances are high that there will be unplanned opportunities to learn. Ever watch the new person try to handle an irate customer, for instance? There is nothing like emotions to ratchet learning up a notch.

When we pay attention to the ways in which people learn, and match their interests with the organization's needs, the odds of executing a successful development plan increase. Not everyone will be motivated to become the executive director, but again, most everyone takes pride in his or her work and wants to perform well. And it's your job to help people do so, which benefits you, the organization, and the community in the end. The Impact Triangle is clearly at work in leadership development—mindset, relationships, and winning practices.

CHAPTER TWENTY-NINE

MANAGING PERFORMANCE

OH, FUN DAYS! If we just didn't have personnel issues, things would be so much simpler. It takes time to be a great and effective supervisor. Who knew? But let's say you hired great employees, conducted exceptional onboarding, and created solid development plans for all staff. And now everyone can just get on with it, right?

In order for staff to perform well and achieve stated goals, you both need to be on the same page in terms of performance expectations, what will be measured, and what you can expect from each other throughout the process. Open communication, clear standards, and performance monitoring are necessary to succeed.

Communication as the Cornerstone

Forbes printed an article by Meghan Casserly on January 2, 2013 entitled "The Top Five Reasons Employees Will Quit In 2013." It states that there has been a bit of a shift in terms of what employees are looking for since the recession: "Now it's about going to a place that has its act together and can offer both long term potential and stability. That's far and away what people are looking for the most." In addition to stability, the compensation package and being treated with respect are at the top of the list, according to Casserly. As a supervisor, notice how much influence you have over an employee's satisfaction rate. Developing staff and managing them well are key ingredients.

What have you done lately to determine how your staff members are motivated? If you don't want a revolving door with employees going out as fast as they come in, it makes sense that you will focus on building strong relationships with staff (one of the cornerstones of the Impact Triangle). And key to any relationship is communication. I don't know that you can lead, inspire, or teach without being an effective communicator. Here are some ways to increase your effectiveness when communicating with staff about their motivation and performance toward goals.

Communication occurs when the message you've sent has been understood by those receiving it. And this can get tricky—did they understand the message you intended to send, or did they hear/read something else?

The art of active listening is of utmost importance. This means you will ask open-ended questions, sometimes several of them, to ensure that you were clearly understood. And you will ask your employees to reflect back a summary of what they heard. It is a very effective way to ensure understanding.

Let's look at some example of substantive open-ended questions. When leading a team, you can ask:

- ► What are you most excited about on this project?
- ► How will we be sure we have enough resources?
- ► How do you feel about the timeline?
- ► Who should we recruit to the team and why?
- ► How do you think you performed to goal?

Some of these questions could launch a juicy discussion that leads to discovering new things about your staff. Others will spin off more questions, because you need to go deeper. As you strive to understand your employees' meaning, it's absolutely critical to reflect back a summary of key points. They will correct as needed.

I think one of the toughest things to remember as a supervisor is to ask employees to summarize key points after *you* have answered questions to confirm what they understood you to say. Great discussions are only as good as what we interpret, retain, and act upon later. So check your perspective on what type of commitment you have to communicating well, and see what you might change.

A word about modalities. How you communicate in person, by phone, and by email will be different. At least they *should* be different. In person, one can see your body language and nonverbal cues, which is how we understand the majority of the meaning of the message. In fact, "psychologists say that a person's impact depends 7 percent on what is said, 38 percent on how it is said, and 55 percent on body language" (Shalleck-Klein, 1998).

Holy cow! If only a small percent of understanding comes from actual words, then what happens when I talk to someone on the phone? At least then the person can hear my tone of voice and inflection. Where do Skype and videoconferencing fall in this equation? And it's frightening to think what happens with email messages!

Here is the takeaway: Essential information is most appropriately handled in person. Facts and short messages are fine for email. But as a supervisor you would be remiss in trying to convey a critical message, such as letting an employee know you are disappointed in his or her performance, by email or text (and I have seen this happen). So it would be time well spent to assess how you are communicating, and determine if you might be able to adjust your approach in order to build strong relationships with your employees, especially when clarifying expectations. In other word, focus on the Impact Triangle.

What Are They Really Supposed to Do?

How will we know our employees are actually performing well? Let's talk about performance standards, which are "benchmarks against which actual performance is measured," according to businessdictionary.com. Now, that doesn't sound so scary, but it's fascinating to see how folks respond to the idea of them. I think it's worth trying to demystify the use of these standards.

Performance standards are actually an asset for employees. Without them, expectations are vague and commonly misinterpreted because there is no specific outcome communicated. Take the program director example and the area of financial management. This is a key performance area as listed on the job description, but what does success look like?

There could be a few performance standards that relate to this area.

- ▶ One could be that person is expected to develop the annual budget with a zero balance according to the timeline.
- ▶ Another could be that he or she monitors the budget and takes corrective action to ensure a balanced budget by year end.

It is now pretty clear what is expected because there are measurable standards in place. (You probably are familiar with the SMART acronym; if not, research it and it will likely be helpful.) Otherwise, just reading that you are expected to develop and manage a budget could leave a lot to the imagination. I can just picture that performance review: "But you never told me..."

It's important that each person in the same position be evaluated by the same standards. It is also good practice to have employees develop these standards with the supervisor whenever possible. However, different people get hired at various times for the same position, and you won't recreate standards every time a new person comes on board.

Certainly an annual standards review with staff makes sense. The goal here is to develop ownership and create conversation about expectations. This is an opportunity for clarification, answering questions, and uncovering what the employees feel they may need in order to succeed.

Performance Monitoring and Feedback

Now that specific expectations are clear, you will want to set people up for success. I once had an employee tell me the best thing I ever did for her was to be accessible. That was a wonderful lesson for me that I always tried to keep in mind. Your team needs you for various reasons, at various times, and to varying degrees.

Support, feedback, and encouragement are important to provide to staff. You cannot just leave them alone and expect them to attain goals. How and when feedback is provided will determine its effectiveness. Think about what you know about your employees and choose a specific feedback strategy for each person.

- First, I want to note that feedback is just information. You are providing facts about what you have observed about employees' behavior. Nothing more, nothing less—there is no judgment involved. When feedback is sincerely provided as a way to help employees succeed, it can influence performance in a positive way.

- Supervisors who learn to relate feedback to a goal, or the big picture, are the most successful at performance monitoring. When an employee understands *why* a particular behavior is required, it is more likely that he or she will work to improve. Otherwise, there is no intrinsic motivation to perform well. Most people want to be successful and take pride in their work, so try to help them make that connection. Be sure they know you are counting on them to deliver the mission.

- Timing is important here. Whether you intend to provide constructive criticism or congratulate an employee on a job well done, think about when your feedback will be most effective. You don't want to inform employees of a shortfall in front of others, but you also don't want to wait too long or the poor performance could continue until it's so far off course, it will be difficult to correct. Conversely, if you wait too long to congratulate someone for excellent performance, the meaning will be lost and the praise will lose its effectiveness.

- For most employees, you will need to give a balance of positive and negative feedback. If you are constantly telling staff what a fabulous job they are doing, it implies they have nothing to learn and actually can serve as a demotivator. They may start to just go through the motions, and performance will suffer.

- On the other hand, if you give only negative feedback, they will feel as if they can't do anything right, and performance will continue to suffer. It's like the parent who asks the child who got all A's except one B why she got a B. Sometimes we need to let the little things go and focus on the big picture.

- Regardless of when and what type of feedback you are providing, be specific. General remarks about doing a great job or hoping the person will do better next time don't provide any tangible information to affect change. Point out what you really appreciated, or what the person particularly needs to address. And always remember, this isn't about the person, it's about behavior.

People are constantly learning and growing in their positions. You will refer to their development plans and continue coaching along the way. Each move you make has the potential for building a stronger relationship with staff, and thereby increasing their satisfaction. Your feedback is valuable and can motivate them to continue to lean into challenges in the future.

Recognition

Too often this is an afterthought. You know what matters most to the organization. So when you have staff doing amazing things, are you prepared to recognize them for it? Typically, we do okay with informal recognition. We say thank you, pat employees on the back, and offer casual acknowledgments of good work. But have you considered putting a bit more structure to it?

You don't have to make it complicated, but it might be worth a conversation with your leadership team to identify a few ways to regularly reward success. For example, you could reward employees who provide the highest level of service, or are exceptional problem solvers, or recruit program volunteers, or are amazing team players.

How you acknowledge great performance can take many forms. Keep your budget in mind. You can present gift certificates, or give public recognition in newsletters, or perhaps give out formal awards. When you are intentional about recognition, you demonstrate thoughtful appreciation.

Performance Reviews

There should be no surprises during a performance review. The employee should have already heard from you where they are excelling and where they may need some more development. But a review is much more than just an assessment of performance.

Let's look at the components of a review:

▶ **Preparation.** Whatever system, timeline, or forms your organization has for the appraisal process, be professional. Throughout the year, you have set clear expectations, coached, and given feedback. Collect the notes from those discussions and be sure to provide a fair assessment of the entire time period, not just the recent history you can easily remember. You may be surprised at the progress made over time.

▸ **Appraisal.** When done well, I have found this to be the shortest part of the meeting. There just aren't any surprises. Acknowledge performance to goals, and point out any deficiencies. Explain the rating system, and if applicable, do a big happy dance and celebrate the employee's raise!

▸ **Goals.** Discuss the future. This is a two-way conversation. You will have some clear objectives in mind, but this is another opportunity to ask questions about what excites people when they look forward; what do they think about the direction of the organization? How can they best support the key initiatives? What else might they need to be successful in their job?

▸ **Development plan.** Have the current copy with you, and dust it off to update it based on the previous part of your conversation. Keep the 70-20-10 learning model in mind, and brainstorm with employees about how they can best position themselves for success. Then commit to strategies and a timeline for implementation.

When you look at how you approach the performance review process, you can see whether you embrace it as an opportunity to build stronger relationships with your staff or have been treating it as a chore to cross off your list. What is your mindset?

Corrective Action

Some people simply are not going to be the right match for the job. You may have worked hard with them, giving wonderful direction and support, but it just isn't working out well. Sometimes this happens, despite your best efforts. Every organization should have a progressive discipline policy, so be sure you are familiar with it. The legal requirements vary among states, so I won't go into much detail—check with your HR specialist to ensure you act within the parameters of the law, and your company's policy, if you need to take corrective action.

And before you take any step, bear in mind that every person, regardless of the circumstance, deserves respect. Keep emotion out of the situation and focus on the behavior that occurred. It is never personal.

Here is some protocol to consider:

- Typically, corrective action begins with some type of verbal warning. This is a firm reminder as to why certain protocol is in place, and a conversation about how the employee needs to improve performance and meet expectations. It is wise to document the conversation, even if your company doesn't require a copy for the employee's personnel file.
- The second time around, a written warning is given and put into the employee's file. At this point, the person needs to recognize his or her employment could be in jeopardy.
- Depending on the number of steps your organization requires, the next step could be another written warning, suspension, or termination. In any case, the situation has elevated to being pretty serious, and it's time to ask questions about whether the person is enjoying his or her work. Sometimes if you give an employee an "out," the person will take it and be rather relieved. Many times there is something else going on that is affecting the employee's performance. Maybe the person just isn't that into you; social organizations aren't for everyone.
- There are some cases in which you will decide to move right to suspension or termination. If someone is accused of stealing, for example, you may want to launch an investigation and suspend the employee with pay during that time. Again, check with HR. At the Y, if a lifeguard fell asleep, which is a matter of life and death, he or she was sent packing immediately. So understanding the practical application of your rules is important. You don't want to put yourself or the organization in jeopardy.

Have you had to fire anyone yet? The experience is not fun, and it can be very humbling. Even when there is no doubt that it is the right thing to do, it can make you wonder if there was a way it could have been avoided. But the "if onlys" do not serve us well. If there is a lesson, learn it and move on with your remarkable team.

Managing performance can be tricky, and frankly exhausting at times. However, think of the Impact Triangle and outline your plan for management early to save time and effort along the way.

CHAPTER THIRTY

STAFF SUCCESSION PLANNING

BACK IN THE SECTION on board development, we talked about succession planning for volunteer leadership positions. For employees, the concept is the same. And the impact is even more significant, as these are the people who are delivering the mission on a daily basis. I won't repeat content here, so refer to chapter 17 as needed. Let's notice the additional benefits:

- Avoid uncertainty and instability
- Provide professional and personal growth opportunities
- Retain talented individuals
- Ensure continued progress toward goals
- Identify competency gaps among team
- Provide leadership continuity
- Be more nimble and flexible to manage adversity
- Energize and build excitement for the future
- Secure a known entity that reduces risk
- Reassure the team
- Save money!!

If you are a board member, it is your job to ensure there are enough resources provided to support succession planning. If you are staff, it's your responsibility to develop and implement the plan. While it may take a fair amount of time and effort up front, the return on that investment is well worth it. So trust the process, believe, and line up some colleagues to help you work on it. It can be eye-opening to realize the potential you have within the organization. And succession planning is a bit different for staff than it is for volunteers. We'll focus on those differences here.

What Do You Need?

This part is the same…in order to identify the right people for the right spots, you must understand what you need. Developing a leadership profile for each position, one that aligns with your strategic goals, comes first. This applies even if you have a small organization that is run mostly by volunteers and just a few paid staff positions. These positions should have a simple, yet thoughtful, list of characteristics you are looking for in an ideal candidate. (Refer to chapter 17 for details on a leadership matrix.)

Keep experience in mind. Would you want someone without supervision experience to lead a large group of employees? Staff development strategies are closely aligned with your goals here. If a current employee would likely perform well in the role, except for the supervisory function, look for opportunities for that person to learn how to be an effective supervisor so he or she will be prepared when an opportunity presents itself. The traits you're looking for should be linked to the organizational goals of your company.

Examples of staff competencies, attributes, or experience could include:

- ► Managing or initiating change
- ► Motivation toward results
- ► Being an effective decision-maker
- ► Commitment to mission and values
- ► Managing conflict
- ► Experience working with volunteers
- ► Leading teams

- Promoting inclusion
- Being a strong communicator/listener
- Influencing
- Project management expertise
- Commitment to personal growth and development

You get the picture. Whatever format you use to create a matrix or chart to track these competencies, you will need to be very clear on what traits will get you the desired result of an exceptional employee.

Do You Already Have It?

As with volunteers, you need to assess whether there are people within the organization who align with the leadership profile. Involving staff in this assessment can in itself be a development opportunity. When they participate in the process, it is a big step toward owning the results.

Keep in mind that you also need to determine if those people are interested in assuming a different position. Just because you see potential in them doesn't mean they feel it is the right match. Perhaps they are very satisfied in their current role and would prefer to master it.

Although you do not want to guarantee a position to anyone, it is motivating to employees to know that they are seen as having potential and are being groomed for leadership roles. I think this also lends itself to a team culture in which staff can support one another in their professional development. A word of caution: Every employee deserves a development plan; a team culture will go downhill fast if there are a few people left out and feeling left behind. Be sure to treat everyone fairly.

Once you have identified who may be strong candidates for succession, you can utilize any number of assessment tools that are adequately objective. These could include:

- **Personality assessments.** These are particularly helpful when a desired trait is the ability to work with diverse groups. And frankly, in today's global economy, with the reality of four different generations active in the workforce, managing diversity should be an expectation. Talking through the results, and the implications for how to work with other personalities, is a nice way for staff to learn about themselves and analyze their communication style.

▸ **A 360-degree feedback process.** It is not uncommon for people to have an incomplete idea of how others perceive them. A 360 process gathers anonymous feedback from the people who work around an employee. This typically includes the employee's supervisor, peers, and direct reports. By gathering this feedback, the person can gain a better understanding of their impact on others. Since effective teamwork is a common expectation in nonprofits, this process can provide insight and better position a person for success. We already know how important relationships are to the Impact Triangle, and when executed well, a 360 feedback tool can be very effective in strengthening critical relationships.

▸ **Information from past performance reviews.** This can be helpful in assessing an employee's readiness for a different position. At a glance, you can see where a person has excelled and where there is room for improvement. The reviews will also indicate if learning has occurred over time or if a person is stuck at the same level of performance.

Whatever combination of assessment tools you use, you must communicate clearly to the employees, including an explanation of how the information will be used. Regardless of the results, all employees should expect to receive an individual development plan to help them grow and develop within their current role, as well as to prepare for any potential future roles.

Bonus Tip: As you prepare the up-and-comers for new roles, bear in mind that they may choose to lead differently than you do. Typically, younger managers prefer collaborative environments. Hierarchy may not have much value to them. Savvy leaders these days are expecting to telecommute a portion of their work week, or perform most of their work in teams. They also seem more in tune with balancing work and the rest of life—good for them! And if you plan to promote baby boomers, get clear on what they value in the work environment, as your assumptions may be wrong.

So as you are coaching, and creating development plans, you would be wise to keep these things in mind. Times have changed.

Is It Working?

As you know, evaluating results is an important step. I recommend conducting an assessment annually to measure results. Ask yourself some questions, such as:

- Did you achieve the percent of inside promotions you desire?
- Has staff retention increased?
- How has staff satisfaction and communication changed, if at all?
- Did the training and development work?
- Did you identify the right folks?
- Do you need to adjust the leadership profile?

Again, outline some key questions around the metrics that matter, and rate the process. Then adjust the plan accordingly to get the best results.

At the end of the day, some of your best people are going to move on regardless of your best efforts to retain them. You cannot control all facets of a person's decision-making. So be prepared to sustain a high level of performance and morale through a transition by having a thoughtful, talent-focused succession plan. Find the right mindset and focus clearly, put the right people in place, utilize best practices to implement the plan, and your team will drive success.

Summary of Key Points

1. The benefits of staff development include improved performance, a more satisfied and proud staff team, increased staff retention, the ability to delegate, a reputation for investing in staff, and a strong candidate pool when there is a vacancy.

2. Professional development is the process of attaining new skill and knowledge with a goal of increasing competency in a culture of lifelong learning.

3. Employees are responsible for their own development, and supervisors create opportunities for learning.

4. Desired competencies must be identified first, and then current staff members are objectively assessed to determine readiness for a new position.

5. Adult learning theory contends that 70 percent of learning is experiential, 20 percent is through coaching, and 10 percent is from formal training.

6. Coaching is a skill that plays a key role. My DIAL method will take you through the stages of discovery, identifying possible solutions, taking action, and learning by review.

7. Communication is essential to managing relationships with staff; active listening is an important skill to master.

8. Performance standards, the specific benchmarks against which performance is measured, are critical for clarity of expectations.

9. Feedback is an integral part of performance monitoring. It is information based on observed behavior that depends upon timing, specificity, connection to goals, and a balance of positive and negative feedback for successful results.

10. A simple, structured recognition plan to reward good performance is valuable.

11. Components of a performance review include thorough preparation, the appraisal, goal-setting, and review of the development plan.

12. Corrective action is a progressive process that must follow your company's HR rules.

13. Succession planning has even more benefits for staff than for volunteers.

14. When outlining a succession plan, develop a leadership profile, use several methods of assessing current staff, utilize development plans, and continue

to evaluate the process to determine if your methods are achieving the desired effect.

Action Steps

1. Evaluate how you currently invest in staff development; get real by asking some of your trusted employees, too.

2. Spend a week with a heightened awareness of how, when, and what you communicate with your staff. Is it the best you can do, and is it what they deserve?

3. Outline some steps to take in the next thirty days to ensure you are a great leader, and then tell an accountability partner who can support your plan. These can be small, incremental things. Rome wasn't built in a day.

PART SIX

THE BENEFITS OF THE IMPACT TRIANGLE... AND THE REAL SECRET

6

CHAPTER THIRTY-ONE

TAKING VACATION DURING PEAK SEASON

I DARE YOU! I know, you're shocked and appalled at the very idea! Of course you are. Because you can just picture it—you fly off to Hawaii right as the annual campaign kicks off, and things instantly become a disaster. No one knows what to do, the materials aren't produced, the organizational structure has just evaporated, and no one is soliciting gifts. What a train wreck! Well, if that's what you envision, that is what will happen.

Or you can choose a different scenario. I did, and guess what? It worked. I literally went to Hawaii during week two of a very intense five-week campaign and completely unplugged. I did not call in, check emails, or otherwise monitor progress. And when I got back, the team was actually ahead of pace! More than eighty volunteers were positioned to raise over $250,000. Why? Because we planned well and educated and supported the volunteer workforce in advance. We sincerely believed it could be done, and we developed strong relationships with the people involved.

And I really wasn't anxious about it while I was gone…well, I admit I thought about work a couple of times, but I didn't get freaked out about it. I felt very confident in the team's ability to make things happen, and they didn't disappoint. Of course, they weren't doing it for me, but as executive director, let's face it—I was largely accountable for the success of their efforts.

Confession: I couldn't have done that a few years earlier. I worked hard to put the right people, with the right attitudes and mindset, in place. And I developed, and revised, and revised again, the training materials and methods of educating everyone involved. I tell this story because to this day people tell me they have never heard of such a bold move, and they are amazed it could work. The power of the Impact Triangle is real and profound.

No organization is dependent on just one person. It takes a village, and your village deserves to be well taken care of and respected for what they know and can accomplish. Once equipped, they can do extraordinary things.

One of the most rewarding things you can witness is observing the leadership that emerges in these kinds of situations. People want to be part of a winning team and will step up when called upon to do so. They will rise to the expectation when you need them the most.

This transformation will move your social enterprise forward in a way that can accelerate your impact very significantly.

The Real Secret

You have a choice. In order to move forward, you need to choose a path. You can choose to believe in your ability to learn. You can choose to surround yourself with people who genuinely care about the mission of your organization, and therefore are committed and generous. You can choose to implement winning practices and utilize tools that will position you for success, even though it may be challenging or new and different. You can choose to do things others don't.

Or not.

My hope for you is that you embrace the concept of the Impact Triangle and start planning how you will shift your mindset to implement it. At least be curious, and keep in mind that if you commit to the Impact Triangle, you will greatly enhance your ability to impact the community and affect real change.

It has been an honor to write this book for you. And many thanks for the work you are doing in the social sector to strengthen the community. The world needs you, and you are the right person for the job.

Let me know how it goes.

AS THE FOUNDER AND PRESIDENT of Create Possibility, Cindi teaches leaders of socially-focused organizations how to grow their business so they can accelerate impact in the community. She knows how it feels to be overwhelmed or frustrated, and needing more direction to advance the mission. Cindi helps executives and board members learn how to look through a different lens so they can serve more people by planning effective strategies that focus on what actually matters most. The challenge could be raising more money, developing an engaged board who truly leads, assembling a motivated, productive staff team, or taking back control so the team can focus on priorities. She has been there and has done the work to figure out the solutions.

Pulling from her experience of leading nonprofits across the U.S., Cindi provides strategy consulting, keynote speaking services, trainings, retreat facilitation, and executive coaching. Throughout her career she has won awards for program development, fiscal management, leadership and fundraising. She has served as a member of the executive leadership team for the YMCA of San Diego County, the second largest Y in the country. Cindi learned first-hand how to navigate the pain points of operating nonprofits and achieve remarkable results.

Cindi is an avid snowboarder, beach jogger, Philadelphia sports fan, and is crazy proud of her son, Corey.

To schedule Cindi to speak at your event, customize a seminar, facilitate a retreat, support you through coaching, or discuss other strategic projects, you can reach her through her website at www.possibility-cp.com

16579649R00127

Made in the USA
San Bernardino, CA
10 November 2014